LILIES

LILIES

Their Care and Cultivation

MICHAEL JEFFERSON-BROWN

CASSELL

Cassell Publishers Limited
Artillery House, Artillery Row
London SW1P 1RT

First published 1990
British Library Cataloguing in Publication Data

Jefferson-Brown, Michael 1930–
Lilies.
1. Gardens. Ornamental wild flowering plants. Cultivation
I. Title
635.9′676

ISBN 0-304 31969-4

Produced by Justin Knowles Publishing Group
9 Colleton Crescent, Exeter EX2 4BY

Editor: Roy Gasson

Line illustrations: David Ashby

Typeset by Keyspools Ltd
Printed and bound in Hong Kong

CONTENTS

LIST OF PLATES

INTRODUCTION

What other garden flowers have the glamour of lilies? They are almost too well endowed with dramatic beauty and immense diversity. Who can fail to admire them? But maybe that is not the question that immediately arises. Perhaps the reaction is more likely to be: 'Lilies are gorgeous, but they are not for me?' They look so wonderful and exotic, they must surely be difficult. They are plants only for the horny-handed gardener with long years of experience and only for the rich, because such plants have got to be expensive? If this is the thinking, it is certainly wrong. The lily now is a plant for everyone, reasonably priced, and easy to manage even for those without a garden. Most modern lilies are among the easiest of plants to grow. They are also among the most rewarding.

This book aims to cover the history and the cultivation of the lily; it describes the wide choice of exciting modern hybrids while not ignoring the wonderful wild species, from many parts of the world, from which they have been derived. Some of these are as easy to grow as the hybrids, but some can test the skills of the clever cultivator who enjoys a challenge. Propagation is an enjoyable part of lily cultivation; there is a variety of methods ranging from the natural division of bulbs to tissue culture, something that need not be beyond the scope of the hobbyist gardener.

Availability of bulbs for gardeners varies. Some species are easily bought, others are rarely for sale but may be reared from seed obtained from specialist traders or from members of lily societies. Turnover of lily hybrids can be rapid, because novelties are the lifeblood of the nursery trade. For the nurseryman it is almost axiomatic that new is better than old, but it is not necessarily so. However, new kinds may be bought with confidence; it just is not worthwhile propagating any new cultivar that is not at least as good a grower and as exciting-looking as existing kinds.

The aim of the book is to persuade more people to join the rapidly expanding numbers of those delighting in their garden lilies. There can be no excuses for denying yourself such enjoyment!

I

THE LILY TODAY

It is the day of the lily. Never before have so many been grown. It is a hugely popular flower. All the signs are that it will continue to gain in favour as the seasons pass. This is no nine-day wonder; no over-promoted stock waiting for a crash. It is a plant that is ideally suited to the present-day skills of growers and hybridizers. It so happens that its metabolic needs are just the kinds that can be perfectly served by modern technology. The lily and the computer may seem an unlikely match, but it is one from which the flower lover is benefiting and will benefit more in the future. This is the most exciting time to start growing lilies. Some of the wild lilies are likely always to be difficult plants, demanding conditions that are not easy to reproduce in cultivation, but the armies of new hybrids that are marching on to the scene are easy plants.

The Lily Population Explosion

In every continent the numbers of lilies being grown are increasing quickly. Vast quantities are being sold as cut flowers and it is this trade that is underpinning the wholesale explosion in lily production. To provide cut flowers economically, stocks of bulbs must be quickly and cheaply supplied. It is here that the lily scores so heavily. A single bulb may be turned into many hundreds and thousands in a very short period. Bulb scales provide young bulbils in a matter of a few weeks and these can be grown on to flowering size in a matter of months rather than years. Some important cultivars can be persuaded to provide bulbils all up the stem in the leaf axils. One stem could provide a hundred bulbils. Some species may be grown from seed to flowering within one growing year. One pod may contain up to a hundred seeds. There need be no shortage of stock to meet the increasing demand for lilies.

Lilies grown under controlled conditions under glass respond very favourably to such culture and huge numbers can be grown in a limited space. Computers can be used to control temperature, moisture, humidity, shading, and ventilation. Human beings check the controls, take preventive action against any pests and diseases, and harvest the results.

Cut-flower Production

It takes fourteen weeks to produce a flowering stem from a newly planted bulb. In theory a greenhouse may produce three crops of flowers a year. There are always bulbs available, as stocks are held in cold storage awaiting their turn. Lilies produce good flowering stems off quite modestly sized bulbs and, since plants may be grown quite close to each other, good use is made of expensive greenhouse space. All the year round, lilies are just as much part of the scene now as chrysanthemums. Stocks come into bloom evenly and may be cut, bunched, brought to market, sold to a florist, and installed in someone's living room in a matter of two days or less. They may be cut and kept in cool storage for a few days waiting for the right market. The demand for the flowers is ever present, the supply is almost as assured; around 200 million stems of lilies are sold each year in the Dutch flower market at Aalsmeer.

Hybridization

All types of lilies are being hybridized in many parts of the world. Amateurs and professionals are engaged in the endless pursuit of ever-better and more diverse types. It is the importance of the cut-flower market that is dominating the interest of the professional breeders. The ideal market flower has precise specifications. First, the flowering stem should be of manageable size – Trumpet lilies 6ft (1.8m) high have a limited appeal. Foliage and stems need to be strong, tidy, and resilient. Flower buds need to look attractive and not be liable to breaking off. Colours of the flowers need to be pleasing.

Two main classes of lilies are attracting the greatest attention from breeders: the Asiatic hybrids, of which the orange 'Enchantment' has been the longtime standard bearer, and the Oriental group, of which the Japanese *Lilium auratum* and *L. speciosum* are the two main founder species. In number the Asiatics are clear leaders, and among these it is those with upward-facing flowers that are most in demand for the cut-flower market. They look right in the florist's window, they scarcely need any arranging by the purchaser, they are immediately attractive in colour and pose, and they last well. The grower can manage their growing and marketing very much more easily than kinds that produce outward or downward-facing flowers.

Gardeners and the Lily

The gardener has had a long-term love affair with the lily, which has so much to offer. It has the advantage of many bulbs in that it grows afresh each year and from a standing start looks always sparkling new. Until the flowers have faded the story is one of continual action – buds burst through the ground and start growing upward at a most satisfying and exciting rate. All is promise and looking forward. Flower buds appear, swell, begin to colour, and burst, amply to justify the eager anticipation. Blossom, of species or hybrid, is splendid. Even after the flowers have faded and the stems and foliage lose their liveliness, the seed pods swell and take on the sculptured forms of classical urns so that they look impressive in their passing. New orange seed contains the miracle of life, the pods now drained of sap are a pale strawy buff, an amalgam of life and death.

And what a generous spirit is here. A stem of *L. regale* or of a hybrid Pink Perfection may have ten, twenty, or over thirty huge trumpets to proclaim their message, a happy proclamation made more completely persuasive by the intoxicating perfume. Some American and Asian species can be almost ridiculously prolific in bloom – stems with over a hundred flowers are possible.

The Lily's Diversity

Diversity covers the whole spectrum of the lily's activities. Bulbs are of different forms and habits. Heights vary from 6in (15cm) to 8ft (2.5m). Flowers vary in pose and form, facing up, out, or down, being narrowly trumpet-shaped, more open, bell-shaped, pointed stars, or with petals recurving backward in extreme cases to form balls. Colour ranges are wide. There are no gentian-blue lilies, but almost every other colour is present. Greens, limes, ivories, whites, all shades of yellow, orange, and red can be found. Some are so deep toned as to suggest black. Dark aubergine colours at one end of a tone scale give way bit by bit to mauves and rosy pinks and blush whites. Many colours are displayed in exciting and unusual combinations – some flowers are a medley of pastel shades, others may be plain coloured but enlivened by dramatic dark beauty spots.

Lilies have many roles to play in the garden. Some are small enough for the rock garden. Many are ideal companions of shrubs or look well in light woodland, while many popular kinds bring distinction to the mixed borders and beds of the modern garden. *L. martagon*, *L. pardalinum* and *L. pyrenaicum* may be planted in the wild garden and left alone for five, ten, fifty or a hundred years. Different kinds will be in bloom from spring to late autumn. By growing bulbs under glass in the conservatory and greenhouse the flowering season can be further extended. Container-grown bulbs can sit on the patio and link house and garden.

No bulb makes such an easy or satisfactory pot plant as the lily. It will grow well and fast in almost any container, provided it has provision made for drainage. Pots as small as 5ins (13cm) can be used, but larger ones are easier to manage. Half tubs are ideal for Trumpet species such as *L. regale* or Trumpet hybrids such as 'African Queen' or Pink Perfection. Containers have the inbuilt advantage that the compost used can be matched ideally to the bulbs' needs. We are not debarred from growing such exciting later-flowering kinds as *L. auratum* and the later still *L. speciosum*, which must have a completely lime-free rooting medium. Having the bulbs in movable containers means that one can give them extra warmth and encourage the bulbs to bloom out of their normal season.

Marketing

Lily bulbs are being produced in many countries. Japan, the home of *L. auratum* and *L. speciosum*, specializes in these types. Oriental hybrids are produced in New Zealand and Australia as well as in the United States of America and Holland. The widest range of kinds is being grown in these last two centres. Specialist growers in Britain are producing interesting kinds. Enthusiasts – amateur, professional, or semi-professional – can be found in most European countries. Holland is producing large quantities of the Asiatics that are used for cut flowers as well as for garden decoration.

Gardeners will normally receive ordered bulbs in the late winter or early spring. Some few specialist growers will supply in the autumn, in time for the bulbs to make good new rooting systems before the winter. No bulb is going to enjoy being planted out in the garden in the winter in cold sodden conditions. Planting when the soil is beginning to warm at the end of the winter or in early spring can be just what is needed. Bulbs get away to a good start.

Sources for garden bulbs are nurseries, garden centres, chain stores, hardware shops, and garage forecourts. Wider ranges of species and cultivars are listed and illustrated in bulb dealers' catalogues. Most European bulb dealers rely on stocks being grown by wholesale growers, probably in Holland, though increasing quantities are being grown in Britain. A few specialist growers list a limited number of bulbs of their own growing and these growers are worth seeking out as they may offer some interesting kinds, while their standard of bulb health and hygiene may be the best. Some of the rare small species, such as *L. mackliniae*, are grown by nurserymen and growers who specialize in small plants. They will not think of themselves as lily experts, but they do a valuable job in conserving stocks of rarities.

Lilies are glamorous and photogenic, and they make ideal items for a mail-order catalogue, or for illustrating prepacks. Prepacked lily bulbs vary greatly in value. Some, packed in polythene bags with wood shavings, can be dried and useless, or even dead, as they hang on hooks in the stores. However, some firms try hard to ensure that customers get reasonable flowering bulbs in good health. They deserve supporting. Bulbs lying in open showcases dry out, so it is best when purchasing these to choose fresh, plump bulbs from a newly opened case.

Flowers are being seen in a wider choice each year at flower shows. It is certainly better to choose the kinds you want from such exhibits than from catalogues; descriptions are necessarily brief and colour reproduction may not do justice to the flower. Naturally, the best way of all is to see lilies growing at commercial centres or in private or public gardens. Here one gets an idea of the character of the whole plant, something that is impossible from a catalogue and often difficult at a show.

Status of the Wild Lily

There are wild lilies in all the continents of the northern hemisphere. They grow in Europe across the Russian landmass to China and Japan; they grow in the Himalayas and bordering countries; a considerable group of species grows in North America. Unhappily there are comparatively few places where lilies are not threatened in the wild. Their position has vastly changed from the beginning of the century. In many places mechanized agriculture has taken a heavy toll, in others it is the pressure of the development of areas for building, industry, and agriculture that has wiped out lily populations. Where there are more people there are going to be the thoughtless ones who will collect or try to collect bulbs. Commercial collecting in the past has done severe damage. Too often we wake up to what is happening too late to do anything to stop the exploitation, desecration, and impoverishment of our environments.

The Lily in the Garden

Garden lilies are now by and large the hybrids. Some few dedicated fanciers grow a number of species and find these fascinating and sometimes challenging. Species are important for their inherent character and beauty. They may have a role to play in the future plans of hybridists yet unborn. They will feature in a conservation strategy. Some are going to manage to hold their own in competition with any hybrid race for a long time to come. In more naturalistic forms of gardening it is likely that the species may look more fitting than some of the hybrids. *L. pyrenaicum* wins for its earliness. *L. martagon* is right for naturalizing in the wild garden. *L. pardalinum* and its kin may flourish in areas where others would fail.

Hybrid lilies are likely always to have a limited commercial life. Some will last longer than others. The vigour and outstanding value of 'Marhan', introduced in 1891, show no signs of diminishing and after it has made its century it could go on for another hundred years. Competition among the Asiatic hybrids is keener — it would be surprising if most of today's favourites were not superseded in a few decades. On the other hand, some of the Mid-Century hybrids, such as 'Enchantment' and 'Destiny', are still just as good as they were forty years ago.

Forecasting the future may be an amusing pastime but it gains us little. There are no statistics to tell us the present state of sales of bulbs for garden use. The numbers of bulbs of the main sorts grown in Holland can be estimated from some statistics kept there, but this includes all those that are grown for cut flowers and so do not help us at all. Nonetheless, it may be possible to make a reasonable estimate of the types that are most popular with gardeners. Asiatic hybrids clearly lead the field, followed by the Trumpets, and then the Orientals. How much this is determined by the sorts most available for purchase is anyone's guess.

As garden sizes shrink, what is grown comes in for greater scrutiny. There is no room for passengers. Lilies are ideal because they grow tidily and make considerable impact. They mix well with shrubs or herbaceous plants. Different kinds can be used to provide colour from spring until the late autumn. They do not require very much room — even the Martagons and some American species that look their best in numbers can be accommodated easily with other plants growing around. The fact that some types do not like lime in their soils need be no great hindrance — the vast majority of those commonly offered are tolerant of some lime and this tolerance can be easily heightened by the incorporation of plenty of humus in the soil. Even real lime haters like *L. speciosum* can be incorporated into the scheme of things either by building up a raised bed of specially composed compost or by growing them in pots.

American gardeners lead the way in growing plants of all kinds in containers so that they may be brought on stage just when they are at their best, placed in position, enjoyed, and then removed after blooming to make way for the next batch waiting in the wings. A relatively small area used as a nursery could do wonders for the garden through the year. Pots of daffodils and tulips will brighten up the spring months, then their stations may be taken over by the earlier Asiatic lilies, which in their turn may be replaced by later lilies or chrysanthemums.

Patio gardening is of necessity an increasingly popular form. More properties are being built with little or no garden space and yet the need for living plants remains as great or even greater in such surroundings. Lilies can provide the colour to mix with more permanent shrubs for many months of the year. They are easier to manage than even daffodils or tulips.

The Future

Ease of propagation and of hybridization virtually ensures that the lily is going to remain in the forefront of the flower parade for the foreseeable future.

Raising fresh plants is at the heart of gardening, perhaps the most satisfying aspect of it. And, if one is raising plants, there beckons the possibility of hybridizing to try to bring some new and even more beguiling beauty into the world. This can be done on whatever scale suits. A single pod may provide winning kinds. The variety of types is such that there are always going to be opportunities for small-scale raisers as well as for the professionals who number their annual sowing of seed by the million.

2

THE LILY YESTERDAY

Evolution

It is thought that the prototype plant of the lily group arose somewhere in the Asian landmass. It would have been an upright plant with a round bulb, stems having a few whorls of large leaves, and orange or yellow flowers with thick petals in a starry form. The extant species that is nearest to it is *Lilium hansonii*. The genera *Lilium*, *Nomocharis* and *Fritillaria* all derive from this common ancestor. A certain amount of guesswork together with an examination of the taxonomic and cytological make-up of our current plants, suggests that among the earliest plants to develop from this original were plants with turk's-cap flowers, precursors of the *L. martagon* types, and the North American lilies.

Turk's-cap lilies would have migrated to the east over the land bridge then uniting Asia and America and to the west, as *L. martagon*, over wide tracts to what are now the Balkans. *L. martagon* is a very adaptable species, being able to grow in a variety of soils with wide ranges of pH values and being equally at home at sea level or at quite considerable elevations. Some less adventurous plants, such as *L. tsingtauense*, might have been early established, but probably only in a restricted habitat. *L. tsingtauense* is a Korean species, a dainty little plant with only a single whorl of leaves.

One major departure from initial lily orthodoxy was the abandonment of the whorled form of leaf dress in favour of a less formal, scattered foliage. This would have been done in a divergent manner, one group of plants eventually evolving into the *L. speciosum* and *L. auratum* types in and around

Japan and others beginning to form the Trumpet kinds found in the same region – species like *L. formosanum* and *L. longiflorum*. An earlier movement could have led to *L. henryi*, which would eventually produce the range of Trumpet lilies found in China, Tibet, and Burma, of which *L. regale* is the outstanding garden kind.

The early primitive turk's-cap lilies eventually became somewhat diverse. They produced the *L. lancifolium* (*tigrinum*) and *L. pumilum* complexes and may also have given rise to the more open-flowered *L. dauricum* or its prototype, and to another line that gave *L. pyrenaicum*, as well as the wide-flowered *L. monadelphum* and *L. candidum*. *L. dauricum* settled down as a good species in the east, while the pre-dauricum types that had made their way westward evolved into the European *L. bulbiferum*.

The early effect on lilies of the arrival of man was not profound. In some parts of the world some species became part of the food supply. Particularly favoured were *L. davidii* and *L. lancifolium*, which became a part of the staple diet of the population in parts of China. The distribution of these species may owe much to their use as food plants. In America the Indians made food of some of the lilies, especially the widespread *L. michiganense*. It is thought that even *L. candidum* owes its wide distribution initially to its use as a vegetable and a plant from which ointment was made in Egypt, then in Greece, and finally in the rest of Europe.

At the dawn of European civilization, *L. candidum* was the lily used as a motif on frescoes and vases. It appears in bas-reliefs in Assyrian buildings dated back to 700–800 BC. In ancient Rome the flowers were eaten and used in medicine, but were soon seen as sacred, being used in offerings to the goddesses Venus, Diana, and Juno.

The Romans, who spread the lily throughout Europe, also passed on its religious association to the Christian church. To begin with, *L. candidum* was seen as a flower of heaven, a symbol of purity. It became the sign of St John the Baptist, St Joseph, St Dominic, and St Anthony of Padua, but it was also associated with a number of virgin saints. It was first used as a special flower of the Virgin Mary in Spain, to which the Moors probably introduced the bulbs. García IV, king of Navarre, in 1043 founded an order sworn to unending warfare against the infidel – the Order of Our Lady of the Lily of Navarre. It was reported that a vision had been seen in the city, the Virgin Mary emanating from a lily and holding the infant Jesus in her arms. Members of the order went into battle with the likeness of the lily painted or embroidered on their breasts. The lily was used by artists of the time and throughout the Renaissance; although sometimes assigned to the archangel Gabriel, it became the more common practice to associate it with the Virgin and so it became the madonna lily.

After the fall of Rome it was left to the various orders of monks to spread *L. candidum* across northern Europe. Ever since then it has remained a much-prized plant. For a long time *L. candidum* was the only lily known to cultivation in Britain – or in other countries away from the lily's natural homelands. But by the 16th century a few other lilies were known in Britain. The botanist John Gerard, in his herbal of 1597, lists five species – *L. candidum*, *L. bulbiferum*, *L. croceum*, *L. chalcedonicum*, and *L. martagon*. He makes it sound as though *L. martagon* was a newcomer to gardens. So, too, does John Parkinson, in his *Paradisi in Sole Paradisus Terrestris*, published in 1629, which describes about a thousand plants grown in English gardens. Parkinson, though, knew of three lily species unknown to Gerard – *L. pyrenaicum* and *L. pomponium* together with *L. canadense* from America. Variations were from then on carefully propagated by the Dutch and British growers who led the way in collecting and cultivating lilies. Other species were added at intervals. In the 19th century a number of the Asian species arrived, some of which had only a very limited life in cultivation. Others were longer lasting and became garden favourites – *L. candidum*, *L. martagon*, *L. pyrenaicum*, *L. chalcedonicum*, *L. bulbiferum*, and *L. croceum* remained popular right up until the 20th century. For most people, indeed, the word lily meant *L. candidum*.

The Golden-rayed Lily of Japan

The great event of the 19th century in the gardener's world, as far as lilies were concerned, happened in 1862. *L. auratum*, the golden-rayed lily, was introduced into Europe from Japan. It would surely have become known and grown earlier had it not been for the Japanese policy of keeping their country closed to all foreigners. The new lily was a miracle. Cultivators vied with one another to grow it. The demand for bulbs was huge. The September 1869 issue of *Floral World* enthused:

'*Lilium auratum* is only just beginning to show its true capabilities. Messrs. Standish and Co., of Ascot, have had a plant in bloom during the past month, with a single stem measuring thirteen feet in height, and bearing upwards of a hundred flowers. At the committee meeting of the Royal Horticultural Society, on the 17th ult., Mr Goode, gardener to the Dowager Lady Ashburnam, Melchet Court, Romney, Hants, exhibited a grand specimen, with the main stems nine feet high, measuring an inch in diameter at a foot from the surface of the soil, besides several smaller stems, bearing altogether 152 flowers – a wonderful example of cultural skill.'

Unhappily the stocks of *L. auratum* fell prey to virus and, despite all the artifice of gardeners, the plant, and the lily family as a whole, fell into something of a decline. It seems that it was the practice of gardeners then to feed *L. auratum* rather too generously and too richly; most of the wild *L. auratum* comes from the sides of volcanic mountains in Japan and other places where it makes do on quite meagre fare.

The shadow over the lily family could not last for ever. The greatest period of plant discovery was the second half of the 19th century and the years up until the outbreak of World War I. During this time the search for new lilies was undertaken with renewed enthusiasm. Plant collectors went out to the unexplored countries of China, Burma, and Tibet, and to the Himalayan regions searching for new plants.

E. H. Wilson

One of the most remarkable of these collectors was Ernest Henry Wilson (1876–1930). As a young student gardener at Kew, Wilson was picked as a man likely to become a successful plant collector by the nursery firm of James Veitch and Sons of London. He was sent on his first collecting expedition in 1899. From this trip to China, completed in 1902, Wilson sent back to England all manner of new and interesting plants. He went on five more collecting expeditions to China and Japan on behalf of the Veitch nursery and, later, of Harvard University's Arnold Arboretum. In 1927 he became keeper of this world-famous arboretum, but died in a car crash three years later.

It was a discovery by Wilson that began the revival of the lily's garden fortune. In the autumn of 1904 a Wilson consignment of about three hundred bulbs arrived at Veitch's nursery to be flowered the following year. The new lily was grown as *L. myriophyllum* but in 1912 was given the name *L. regale*. Its vigour, and the ease with which its seed grew rapidly into flowering bulbs, ensured that there was always stock that would be clear of virus. Wilson wrote of the new lily's homeland:

'There in narrow, semi-arid valleys, down which thunder torrents, and encompassed by mountains composed of mud-shales and granites, whose peaks are clothed with snow eternal, the Regal Lily has its home. In summer the heat is terrific, in winter the cold is intense, and at all seasons these valleys are subject to sudden and violent windstorms against which neither man nor beast can make headway. There, in June, by the wayside, in rock-crevices by the torrent's edge, and high up on the mountainside and precipice, this Lily in full bloom greets the weary wayfarer. Not in twos or threes but in hundreds, in thousands, aye, in tens of thousands. Its slender stems, each from two to four feet tall, flexible and tense as steel, overtopping the coarse grass and scrub and crowned with one to several large funnel-shaped flowers more or less wine-coloured without, pure white and lustrous on the face, clear canary yellow within the tube and each stamen filament tipped with a golden anther.'

Before travel became easier it was the writings of Wilson that gave us the best idea of the conditions under which many of the fascinating eastern lilies grow. He castigates the writers about *L. auratum* for giving a false idea of its native stations and the soil in which it grows. It was suggested that the bulbs of this splendid lily grew under a considerable layer of leaf mould. It must have seemed difficult for writers to think of such a splendid thing growing on unenriched soils, but Wilson explained:

'In Japan there is much poor and hungry soil but none more so than the slopes of august Fiji and the volcanic deposits of the neighbouring Idzu province. Around Matsushima, a beauty spot in northern Japan, I saw this Lily in quantity growing in coarse gray sandstone rock. In western Japan, in the province of Uzen, I also met with it growing wild on gravelly banks and hillsides amongst small shrubs and coarse grasses. It is the open, porous soil, and not the rich humus, that this Lily luxuriates in. Leafsoil it loves in common with all Lilies, but it wants no unaerated acid peat and it loathes raw nitrogenous manures.'

The cult of the lily in the first half of the 20th century was dominated by attempts to provide suitable homes for the species. There were a number of hybrids, but their position was almost auxiliary to that of the species. Prices for some of the bulbs were so high as to preclude their very wide cultivation. The supply of stock was somewhat limited, although of certain kinds there was a very good regular supply. Those, such as *L. regale*, that were easily raised from seed, were plentiful and much appreciated. *L. auratum*, imported from Japan, was never cheap. The growing of anything approaching a comprehensive collection was the almost exclusive preserve of the rich. Nursery firms, though, were able to supply many kinds of lilies. W. A. Constable Ltd of Southborough, Kent, grew an extensive range of lilies from all parts of the world and produced a very fine annual catalogue. Its range of wild types has never been rivalled. Dutch growers offered a range of the somewhat more amenable species from the beginning of the century.

The first to raise significant numbers of lilies from seed were the Japanese, who used their native species and kinds that had been introduced from China. *L. dauricum* was one of the most important. A race of lilies was introduced into Europe and distributed by Dutch growers as *L. × maculatum*. They were easy plants with upward-facing flowers, predominantly orange-reds but with some yellows, and really the precursor of the modern Asiatic hybrids.

Jan de Graaff

In the 1930s and 1940s Jan de Graaff began the huge programmes of hybridization that made his name the foremost in the story of the development of modern lilies. He founded Oregon Bulb Farms in 1932, growing many types of bulbs, including daffodils. This was to become the centre of the lily world as he and his team of helpers concentrated all their efforts on work to revolutionize the lily genus. First they collected every possible species and hybrid, then selected out the very best of each to grow on with a view to assessing their potential in programmes of crossings. While other types were not totally neglected, the main emphasis of the work was on the breeding of better Asiatic and Trumpet hybrids and Orientals from the mixed *L. auratum* and *L. speciosum* parentages.

The obvious starting point for the Asiatics was the series of Japanese-raised lilies, *L. × maculatum*. One of these had become well known as a clone called 'Alice Wilson', a lemon flower with red spots. In Holland these maculatums had been crossed with the European species *L. bulbiferum* and had given rise to a race known as *L. × hollandicum* or *L. × umbellatum* (the last name was dropped because

it had been used for an American species). The *L. × hollandicum* series were strong, stout-stemmed plants with shiny rich foliage and firmly held, cup-shaped, upward-facing flowers ranging from yellow to deepest red. In America another species was introduced into the breeding of these hybrids. The cross was *L. × hollandicum × L. lancifolium (tigrinum)* and the resulting progeny was given the name *L. × umbtig*. Whatever one may think of the name, the flowers and plants seemed a distinct advance. None inherited the pendent pose of *L. lancifolium*, but they had better, wider, shallower, cup-shaped blooms and strong stems with smart leaves more or less at right angles to the stem and neatly spaced.

It was the cross *L. × umbtig* with *L.* 'Alice Wilson' that gave Jan de Graaff his first series of Mid-Century hybrids, one of which 'Enchantment', has since been grown in countless millions.

In England, around the turn of the century, a flower had been produced at the Royal Botanic Gardens, Kew, from a white Trumpet species *L. leucanthum* var. *chloraster* crossed with the orange-flowered *L. henryi* with its curled back petals. It was a creamy buff flower named 'Kewense'. Other breeders tried to combine the genetic potential of *L. henryi* with the Trumpet kinds and one or two isolated triumphs were recorded, but it was Jan de Graaff who mounted a full-scale campaign to solve the problem. *L. henryi*, *L. leucantheum* var. *centifolium*, *L. sulphureum* and *L. sargentiae* and a few of the previously successful Aurelian hybrids and 'T. A. Havemeyer' were crossed both ways with *L. henryi*. *L. henryi* was crossed with pollen of the Trumpet species. Huge quantities of seedlings were raised and selecting from these laid the basis for the races of golden, lemon, and orange Trumpets as well as the more wide-open flowers marketed under various category names such as 'Sunburst'.

Hybridizing is today being carried on all over the world. While many types of flowers are being bred, the greatest concentration is on Asiatics that may be suitable for cut-flower production. These are being raised by the million in Holland and a rigorous selection process makes sure the propagated clones suit the various markets worldwide for which they are destined.

3

THE LILY EXAMINED

The Cycle of Growth

Healthy lilies grow with rapidity, far more quickly than the majority of bulbous plants. Some grow from seed to flowering plant in a matter of months, although there are some species, such as *L. martagon*, that may take six years to reach flowering-sized bulbs. Established bulbs get smartly through their annual cycle. Often the shoots do not appear above ground until mid-spring but then make good their late start by shooting up to flowering in two or three months. The lily is a dynamic plant, always on the move.

Seed pods ripen to a straw colour and split open at the top and down the sides of each of the three compartments to reveal the many seeds, flat papery discs, piled up like plates, but light and waiting to be blown away. Seed of different types varies in its weight, some fertile seed being quite light in comparison with that of other species or hybrids. Pods of ripe seed turned out on a sheet of paper will usually be easily seen to be fertile or not – the fertile seed is plumper and if a light is shone through the seed the embryo can be clearly seen. Infertile chaff is easy enough to winnow away.

Ways in which the seed germinates are detailed on pages 113–14. Suffice here to say that there are four classes. The first germinates immediately and pushes up a narrow strap of a leaf, sometimes with the seed capsule still sticking to the tip. The second performs in the same way, but only after a delay. A third class germinates by immediately sending from the seed a tube that descends into the soil for a distance before turning and making for the surface.

Where the tube bends the young bulb starts to develop; the upward movement continues and the first true leaf shows above the surface. The fourth class behaves in the same way as the third, but does so after a delay.

Depending on the type of lily, the first leaf may remain alone throughout the first season, or, in more vigorous types, be joined by a second, third, and more leaves as the season develops. Young bulbs may soon have a small rosette of spear-shaped leaves. As the bulbs grow they will reach the stage of producing a stem with attendant foliage. Now the plant is well on its way.

Bulbs

The bulbous rootstock of the lily is a varied one – each species has its own character. The main difference between it and those of other well-known bulbous plants is that the growing point is surrounded by a number of detachable scales rather than completely enveloping ones such as those of the tulips and daffodils. Another main difference is that, while bulbs such as tulips have their scales enclosed in a coat called a tunic and are described as tunicated, the lily has no such outside wrapping. In some lilies, such as *L. concolor* and *L. pumilum*, the scales are broad and do a conscientious job of wrapping their inner parts, but in some American species, such as *L. pardalinum*, the scales are distributed along the length of the rootstock's stems, like leaves along a shoot, and only at the growing points do they gather together in a slightly more usual approach to an orthodox bulb.

A bulb is a stratagem to hoard resources for next year's growth and can be viewed as a compacted stem with bud. The stem is normally reduced to the cone-shaped basal plate on which the storage vessels, the scales, are arranged, these scales being adaptations of the bases of the leaves. They protect and nourish the central growing point of the bulb until the roots get into full working order. Scales vary considerably in their form. Some overlap widely and approximate to the scales of tunicated bulbs; others are much narrower and looser – these are more liable to damage out of the ground and so permit the incursion of pests and fungus troubles that much more easily. A few Asian species and more of the American ones have their scales distinctly waisted – usually described as 'jointed' – and are liable to break at this weak point. Species having these unusual scales include *L. dauricum*, *L. pardalinum*, *L. philadelphicum*, *L. parryi*, *L. parvum*, and *L. ocellatum*.

Botanists and writers have found it a convenience to distinguish four or five types of bulbs. There is variation within any one of these types. The most important and most obvious type is the commonly seen one, the erect or concentric bulb, in which the scales are more or less tidily arranged around the central growing point like an artichoke. Asiatic hybrids in showcases will be of this type and so will be the more usual Trumpet lilies, such as *L. regale*.

A small group of lilies, although looking quite normal above ground, have bulbs that produce the upright stem that bears leaves and flowers but at the same time project a stem (stolon) sideways at the end of which a new bulb is formed. This stoloniferous bulb habit is most perfectly displayed by *L. canadense*.

Below ground, the American *L. pardalinum* can quite quickly form a permanent mat of freely branching stems, with at the end of each branch a growing point that will provide the base for the above-ground stem. Along the stems of the root-stock the scales are scattered, each pointing upward, but they are closer together at the growing points.

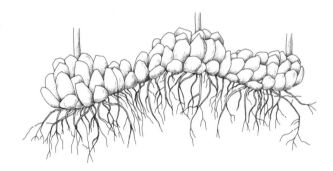

A rhizomatous bulb – for example, *L. pardalinum* or 'Cherrywood'

Some kinds, such as *L. humboldtii*, effect a compromise between the rhizomatous-bulb rootstock form of *L. pardalinum* and the erect, rounded bulb of, for example, *L. regale*. The bulbs of these look like orthodox erect ones that have lurched to one side to produce a further growing point. They are normally termed sub-rhizomatous.

Limited numbers of other species, such as *L. duchartrei*, are really erect, concentric bulbs, but when the stem emerges from the bulb, instead of making straight for the surface, it wanders below ground, perhaps as far as 2ft (60cm). Along this stem at intervals new bulbs are produced, one, two, three, or four, before the stem rises into the air to perform its normal duties. These are the creeping-stemmed bulbs, sometimes called stoloniferous-stemmed bulbs, but this may confuse with the truly stoloniferous types like *L. canadense*.

By far the majority of lilies have straightforward, round, erect, concentric bulbs.

Size, vitality and longevity of bulbs vary hugely. The delicate little American species *L. catesbaei* has

An erect, round bulb – for example, *L. regale* or 'Enchantment'

a tiny apology of a bulb, some few scales clearly made from the bases of leaves and looking as if each had been bitten off at the top. On the other hand, some bulbs can be huge. Those of some Trumpet hybrids can be 8in (20cm) across. Bulbs of *L. auratum* grown for food and lined out like potatoes will grow to several times their normal size.

The metabolism of different types varies. *L. pumilum* is all quick frenetic growth from seed to flowering bulb and will then produce such quantities of seed that it can threaten its own life. If flower heads are nipped off when they have finished blooming, bulbs can be encouraged to take a longer-term view of life. No such measures are needed for kinds such as *L. hansonii* and *L. martagon* that once planted may be expected to keep on growing for perhaps over a hundred years. They will provide plenty of seed and increase tremendously by this means if given the chance, but the original bulbs will carry on growing without check. The most famous British stand of martagons is in the wilderness gardens of St John's College, Cambridge, where thousands of plants create a mauve-pink cloud beneath the trees through the months of June and July each year. They grow in rough grass and have been there for hundreds of years. There are one or two spots in Britain where this same species has gone wild.

Many of the recently bred Asiatic hybrids are strong enough plants but seem to do their best if they are lifted every two or three years and given a fresh position to exercise their energies and display their wares. 'Enchantment' and all the kinds bred since are of this restless persuasion.

Stems, Roots and Leaves

Some lily stems, such as those of *L. pardalinum giganteum* and many of the American species hybrids, rocket heavenward with enormous zest. *L. martagon* is no slouch either, getting under way when the daffodils are in bloom and reaching maximum height in early summer. These stems are perfectly upright and strong. Others may be more slender but still very wiry and resilient. A few, such as those of *L. davidii willmottiae*, will be rather different. Stems tend to emerge at a slope from the bulb and,

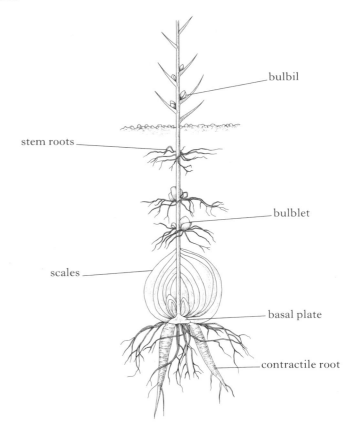

bulbil

stem roots

bulblet

scales

basal plate

contractile root

Parts of the plant

though being more or less upright, will arch over with the weight of their blossom. They will welcome the support of surrounding shrubs as they may have up to a hundred flowers to a stem and although the stem is tough it is rather under-stressed for this type of load.

Stems of *L. auratum*, which can easily reach 8ft (2.5m), are particularly strong. They need this strength to hold aloft maybe some dozens of flowers each 8–12in (20–30cm) wide. This duty is in marked contrast to that performed by some diminutive kinds like the nomocharis-like *L. mackliniae*, the creeping *L. duchartrei*, or *L. concolor*. These slender-stemmed kinds may have only a few blooms, although bolder bulbs will have quite a generous number, but the stems are wiry and adequate.

Below the soil surface many lilies have stems that produce roots. This is rarely the case with European species, but most of the Asians are very active in this way. Just above where the stem arises from the bulb there is often a thick ring of roots that do an important task in supplementing the work of the bulb roots. They nourish the growing plant and help to anchor the stem in the soil. In many kinds further rings of roots can be found, as well as some scattered roots. So efficient are these stem roots that it is quite possible to detach the stem from the bulb and for it to carry on growing normally – the stem roots can easily cope with the nutritional needs of the flowering stem. Alas, sometimes an appearance of health and beauty above ground is totally due to the good offices of the stem roots.

Stems may provide new bulbs. Buds may develop on the stems below the ground or in the open air to give new small bulbs. Most prolific of all is *L. lancifolium* (*tigrinum*) which can grow one or

more bulbil in every leaf axil and end a growing season with a hundred or more bulbils from each stem for the owner to grow on. If the Chinese taste for the cooked bulbs spreads, there should be no shortage of stock to start growing fields full of autumn orange-red. Many of the Asiatic hybrids have the capability of producing such bulbils. By decapitating stems early on to prevent flowering one may induce many cultivars to devote their energies to making lots of bulbils. One, two, or three bulbils can be grown from a leaf axil. Often the smaller stems are more prolific than the strong stout ones. This applies also to some of the creeping-stemmed species like *L. wardii*. The immature-sized bulbs are more likely to send out stoloniferous stems below ground and engender the formation of several more young bulbs along their lengths. The bulbil-forming potential of young plants can be exploited commercially.

Some lilies can be impressive foliage plants, however others are less showy. Leaves are of differing forms and colours and are displayed in various manners. The prototype lily pattern is of a strong upright stem with leaves arranged in whorls at intervals. Narrow, or slightly broader elliptical leaves may number from about eight to around eighteen to a whorl. They are held more or less horizontally and slightly drooping in the case of *L. martagon*, while the rather darker leaves of such Americans as *L. pardalinum* are initially inclined to be somewhat more upright. The total effect of bare stems with whorls of leaves at intervals is stylish. As distinctive in another manner is the foliage of *L. speciosum*. Leaves are broad, pointed ovals with longitudinal veining; they are held by leaf stalks at pleasing angles to the stems and whole plant. In many types the leaves are scattered up the stem, a series of narrow, willow-leaf shapes from the pale to dark purple-green.

The neatness and disposition of the foliage is one of the points that breeders look for when evaluating the worth of some new seedling. The foliage needs to be healthy and look healthy. It needs to be not too crowded and to be held tidily. It looks best with a gloss finish. Some few kinds are less attractive in the way they hold their leaves – *L. pumilum*, for example, tends to have its foliage clasping the stem.

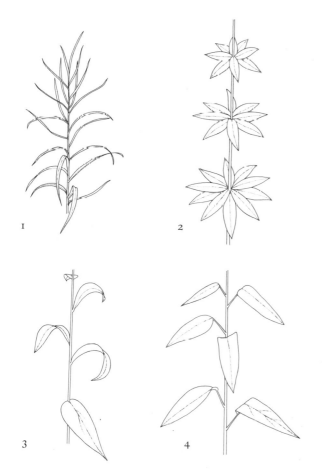

Leaf forms: 1 thin and scattered – for example, *L. pyrenaicum*; 2 whorled – for example, *L. martagon* or *L. pardalinum*; 3 scattered – for example, 'Enchantment'; 4 stalked – for example, *L. speciosum*.

Flowers

Nowhere is the diversity of the genus more obvious than in its flowers – their numbers, arrangements, forms, colourings, poses, sizes, and textures. From one to over a hundred blooms may be displayed on a single stem. A particular bulb of a species such as *L. regale* may have a solitary maiden bloom as a seedling, and then year by year increase its offerings until over twenty are displayed (three dozen is a possibility). I have grown *L. davidii willmottiae* with over a hundred blooms. Some American species, such as *L. parryi*, usually content themselves with from one or two up to a dozen blooms, but will exceptionally produce a stem with fifty or more. *L. henryi* is best known with up to a dozen orange flowers, but growing strongly in well-favoured spots it has been recorded a massive 10ft (3m) high and carrying seventy flowers. Such well-known kinds as *L. martagon*, while settling down, may be content with a pleasing dozen or so but are capable of stems with a pyramidal candelabra of some fifty to sixty curled-up blooms. It is one of the joys of lily growing that there is no knowing just how well some particular kind is going to perform in any year.

Almost every method of display is employed. Some European species, such as *L. bulbiferum*, and some Asian kinds, such as *L. concolor*, have their flowers looking upward to the heavens. Others, such as the madonna lily, face outward. Most of the species favour a more-or-less nodding pose, either hanging completely pendent like the Martagons or at angles like the *L. speciosum* forms. The majority of Asiatic hybrids face upward and this may well be just what we need from plants that grow to about 2ft 6in (75cm) high. Certainly in the border the colour is well displayed. The fact that most were bred with the cut-flower market well in mind is of no matter. At early and mid-summer these extrovert types are at their best. Later, it is the kinds with nodding flowers that take over, save for the magnificent *L. auratum* that upsets all rules and is a law unto itself. If you find the upward-facing kinds just that bit too blatantly extrovert, you have the choice of using the early flowering *L. martagon* kinds and their very useful hybrids with *L. hansonii*.

The simplest arrangement of blossom is in a straightforward umbel looking up, all the flower stems emanating from a single point, as in many Asiatic hybrids. Composite umbels are possible when the flower stems radiate as bouquets from two or three points on the main stem, as may be the case with stronger Asiatic hybrids. More popular among the species is the raceme deployment, by which blooms are displayed on their own flower stalks alternately up the stem. A stage more complex is when composite racemes are employed; the main flowering stem has secondary flowering stems, alternately arranged, with the flowers displayed, also alternately, on these substems. *L. martagon* displays its blooms in a raceme, *L. speciosum* uses a composite raceme.

Flower form may be a simple star with the petals tending to curve a little back so that each petal is somewhat convex. In *L. pumilum* and many others the petals reflex strongly and can end up as balls or cylinders. These flowers with curled-back petals are often described as turk's-caps; because of their supposed likeness to an old-fashioned headdress worn by Turks. Other lilies, such as *L. rubellum* and *L. szovitsianum*, although they have convex petals that recurve somewhat, may be thought of as wide bells. The other main form of the flower is the trumpet shape – sometimes, in some of the eastern species, very elongated. *L. longiflorum* and *L. neilgherrense* are two with long narrow trumpets but with the petals then opening out and recurving so that one does not immediately realize the length of the flower, a length that lends it a particular grace. A few species confound the norm by having

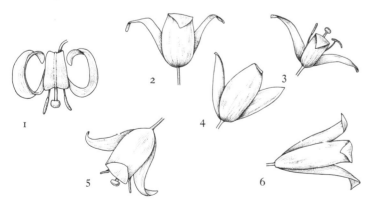

Flower shapes: 1 turk's-cap – for example, *L. martagon*; 2 bowl – for example, 'Matchless'; 3 star – for example, *L. concolor*; 4 cup – for example, *L. bulbiferum*; 5 open trumpet – for example, Golden Splendour; 6 trumpet – for example, *L. longiflorum*.

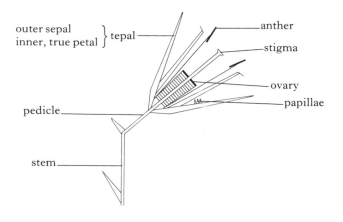

outer sepal
inner, true petal } tepal
anther
stigma
ovary
papillae
pedicle
stem

Parts of the flower

cup-shaped blooms with petals that are concave for most of their length, though the tip may recurve. Such a species is the dainty *L. mackliniae* from the hills on the borders of India and Burma. Some species vary considerably in the flower form. *L. parvum*, while normally a compromise between a bell and a trumpet shape, can be somewhat cup-shaped at times.

Colours of the flowers are governed by the presence or absence of the main pigments carotene and anthocyanin. The yellows and oranges are due to carotene, the greater the concentration the further the colour moves from yellow to orange and red. Anthocyanin governs the pinky mauve colourings and is a water-soluble chemical that is sensitive to light and high temperatures. It can fade and break down in heat. Golden colour appears in the throats of some lilies, the gold normally being genetically inhibited from spilling over into white areas.

The lily family differs from the irises and the amarylids in having its ovary within the flower.

Petals enclose the ovary. These are really three sepals and three petals, the six together sometimes being called tepals. Most gardeners are going to regard them simply as petals but will note that the three outer ones that form the buds may be coloured on the outside differently from the three inner segments. Six conspicuous anthers are held by separate slender filaments balancing just short of the stigma. The stigma is held prominently forward in the centre of the flower, in Trumpet kinds often turning somewhat upward at the end of the style. The stigmas may be large as in the Trumpet species or small as in the Asiatic group.

Petals have nectary furrows toward the centre back, usually coloured a greenish or yellow shade. Some may have hairs. A more unusual feature of some species, especially the *L. speciosum* forms, is the series of raised points on the petals to the centre and rear. These papillae may or may not be coloured. They are particularly numerous in flowers of *L. henryi*, forming a veritable forest for any small insect trying to make its way toward the narrow nectary furrow.

Seed pods develop from fertilized flowers and take on interesting and attractive urn shapes, each pod being brought to an upright position no matter in what pose the flower was originally held. Shapes vary from relatively squat and rounded to elongated, but all reveal the form of the underlying three compartments. These compartments have the flat seeds packed in layers, each pod owning any quantity up to over a hundred. The most usual colour is a rusty beige, but some are paler, with those of *L. martagon album* being a ghostly white. Seeds are distributed by wind as the pods split from the top and slowly crack open to allow more and more to float away.

4

GROWING AND ENJOYING LILIES

Presenting the case for growing lilies must be the easiest brief in the world. Nearly every argument is on the side of the lily; the advocate is almost embarrassed by the amount of positive evidence there is to present. It could be argued that the genus has within it such a diversity of beauty and talent that any one gardener can find a number of lilies suited exactly to his needs. Workaholic business types with only a few seconds to spare can be given a shortlist of types that will thrive with the barest minimum of care. At the other extreme the plantsman can be catered for, the dedicated cultivator who is never quite happy unless struggling with the problems of things vegetable from far-flung corners of the world that require exacting conditions and present a challenge to his horticultural expertise. Yes, there are some difficult lilies!

Fashions in gardening change. Different plots present different problems and opportunities. Here a conventional suburban gardener will struggle to maintain regular order and respectability in a formal rectangular plot with close-clipped grass around borders and beds predominantly herbaceous. All is colourful propriety. The lilies in this garden must be neat, tidy, and bright; we could quickly provide a list. 'Enchantment' would enchant, 'Fire King' would be fiery, and 'Festival' would be festive.

At present there is a movement towards more natural forms of planting; plant communities, interesting contrasts of foliage, happy accidents, all are contrived. The art is to conceal the art. Such unnatural naturalism may find it difficult to place the vivid extrovert lilies such as 'Enchantment', but the list is long of more graceful cultivars that would lend magic to the whole. There are Asiatic hybrids that will charm rather than scream. The North hybrids with pastel-coloured, pendent flowers are the most graceful of the Asiatics, but one could also use the older Martagon hybrids of the Backhouse or similar series to provide just what such a naturalistic practitioner desires.

Whatever the setting, the lily is likely to be the star turn. It is an aristocrat of the floral kingdom. Owners of stately homes, whose gardens cover many acres and seem to be just part of the managed landscape, will be planting lilies maybe with rhododendrons or other shrubs in light woodland. In Britain, Windsor Great Park, Knightshayes, and other great gardens are planted with bold groups of American species, the wonderful *L. superbum*, the strong *L. pardalinum*, and *L. pardalinum giganteum*, together with the magical *L. canadense*, so long grown in Europe but always tremendously exciting and a triumph when it grows well. *L. martagon* is given its candelabra head, and if it seeds, that is as it should be – the wait for the seedlings to bloom in six or seven years is only a short passage in the history of the garden.

At the other end of the scale, the lily can transform a tiny patio. There is not another bulb that will grow as well or as easily in containers. With a little manipulation and careful forethought the patio can become a stage upon which with the lily will exhibit its beauty and grace from late spring until the autumn. Asiatics, Trumpets, Orientals –

they all take their turn and bring exciting life to a concrete or stone-paved world.

One of the attractive features of the lily's character is that many kinds need so little fussing and attention. They will stand considerable neglect. There are, of course, also plenty that can be killed easily. As with many plants, it is a matter of horses for courses, lilies for locations. They need soil, light, moisture, warmth. Even the easiest of kinds will repay care taken to make sure they have all that they require.

Soils

There are no lilies that like a bog. There are one or two species that can be found in marshes and bogs, but they live on tussocks above the sodden mass. Even *L. maritimum*, a Californian species formerly quite widespread in swampy areas near the sea, grew among shrubs a little above the general level and where sand and the roots of its associates kept the soil from stagnant sogginess.

The most basic need of a lily is good drainage. Then one can start worrying about acidity and alkalinity, handily expressed in pH levels. Seven is neutral, figures above show increasing alkalinity and numbers below greater acidity. Much has been made of the difficulty of growing lilies in soils with some lime in them. When the choice of lilies to grow was limited to the species this was of greater consequence. There may have been a need to worry – certainly it would have been prudent to take care that the needs of specific kinds were fairly well matched to suitable soils. There are some wild kinds for which the presence of lime is a death sentence. *L. speciosum* and *L. auratum* are condemned in the presence of lime. On the other hand there are many species that are completely tolerant of lime and some that maybe welcome it. The question of alkalinity is of less importance now that cross-breeding has given us hybrids with a degree of tolerance of lime unknown to their parents. This makes the provision of suitable soils much easier.

As a sweeping generalization it may be suggested that the vast majority of lilies are happiest with the soil just on the acid side of neutral. As most garden soils hover around neutral the provision of this touch of acidity is not difficult. The bulbs of many of the species that may become somewhat queasy with lime can have their tolerance of it dramatically improved by the incorporation of acid-enhancing materials such as well-made composts, well-rotted manures, leaf-mould, and peat.

Specifications of ideal lily soils would include a high proportion of humus, but would also call for a gritty openness to ensure good drainage. Heaven for lilies is such a soil plus a plentiful supply of non-stagnant underground moisture in the growing months but with the resting months of winter being free of excess wet. Many lilies come from hillsides and mountain slopes where the melting snows of spring and summer provide just such a moving underground source of moisture, a supply that may be augmented by rainfall, though in parts this may be entirely absent for some months. This can certainly be the case in areas where some American species grow, where the winter soil is not excessively wet because a thick snow blanket covers the soil through the winter months.

It is surprising how many lilies will do well on soils that are far from being ideal. I grew *L. pardalinum* and *L. pardalinum giganteum* in an orange London clay of a consistency that enabled me to make earthenware pots from it. Drainage was less than perfect. Yet even here it was one of the minor pleasures in life to go each spring to make a census of the number of flowering stems piercing the surface and to calculate just how many more there were than in the previous season.

The most widespread of all lily species, *L. martagon*, has such an undemanding appetite that it will thrive on all sorts of soils. It is certainly tolerant of lime and it may even be the better for it. And if such is the case for the species, then the hybrids are even more amenable.

Lime-tolerant Lilies

Gardens beset with high levels of lime will need a list of those kinds that may be planted with the knowledge that they will thrive. The species are listed overleaf. Other lime-tolerant kinds will include all the hybrids of these species, notably the Martagon hybrids, such as the Backhouse series, *L. × testaceum*, and the Asiatic hybrids derived from species such as *L. bulbiferum*, *L. cernuum*, *L. concolor*

Lime-tolerant Lilies

L. amabile	L. leucanthum
L. brownii	L. longiflorum
L. bulbiferum	L. martagon
L. callosum	L. monadelphum
L. candidum	L. pardalinum
L. cernuum	L. parryi
L. chalcedonicum	L. pomponium
L. concolor	L. pyrenaicum
L. davidii	L. regale
L. hansonii	L. szovitzianum
L. henryi	

and *L. davidii*, as well as the early series of hybrids, which are still sometimes marketed as *L. × hollandicum* and *L. × umbellatum*. The Trumpet hybrids also show a high degree of tolerance, especially if they are given reasonable quantities of humus.

Acid Lovers

There are a few species that, while they manage in neutral soils, prefer an acid environment. Some of the American species are of this order and one such is the curious botanical curiosity *L. catesbaei*, a tiny, dainty plant that shares with the more widespread *L. philadelphicum* the distinction of having upward-facing flowers, all the rest of the American group having pendent blossom to a greater or lesser degree. *L. occidentale*, from the coastline of northern California, a close relative of *L. maritimum*, is another lily that is happy in acid soils. But more importantly horticulturally are the Bellingham hybrids, which do well enough in neutral soils but are happier in acid ones. This leaves the graceful Asian *L. lankongense* and the Orientals *L. speciosum* and *L. auratum* as the remaining kinds that flourish on acid soils. This short list is of the more decided acid lovers – as a generalization one could say all the American species prefer somewhat acid soils.

Sunlight and Shade

Lilies like sun and shade, both at the same time. Like clematis, they would have heads in the sun and toes in the shade. But having said that, many kinds

will be happy enough to sunbathe with little save perhaps a mulch of peat or shredded bark over the soil covering their bulbs. Leading sun-worshippers include *L. amabile*, *L. canadense*, *L. cernuum*, *L. dauricum*, *L. formosanum*, *L. longiflorum*, *L. pumilum*, and *L. regale*. To these species may be added their hybrids and especially the Asiatics, such as the Mid-Century hybrids and plants of similar breeding.

Many modern gardens, being relatively small plots, are likely to have major areas that are at least in partial shade. This need not deter the lily planter. Provided deep forest gloom is given a miss, most lilies will certainly stand a bit of shade. Some are at their very best with the dappled shade of light woodland or more artificial shade. There are types with colours that fade in the full glare of sunlight but will more or less preserve their full tones given the encouragement of some shade. The very hardy *L. henryi* is one that will benefit from some shade. In the open it will grow well enough, but the mid-orange flowers are liable to bleach in sunshine and can begin to look rather anaemic after a few days. Another extrovert hardy type also benefiting from shade is *L. hansonii* often-time marriage partner of *L. martagon*, with tawny-coloured flowers that are definitely the better for keeping out of strong sunlight.

Kinds that will be happy enough in partial shade are listed below. (Some of these lilies have already

Lilies for partial shade

L. amabile	L. lankongense
L. auratum	L. mackliniae
L. bolanderii	L. martagon
L. brownii	L. michiganense
L. canadense	L. pardalinum
L. davidii	L. parryi
L. distichum	L. regale
L. duchartrei	L. rubellum
L. grayi	L. rubescens
L. hansonii	L. speciosum
L. henryi	L. superbum
L. japonicum	L. tsingtauense
L. kelloggii	L. wardii
L. lancifolium	L. washingtonianum

appeared as sun-loving types. This is not a mistake – many lilies are very tolerant.) Other shade-tolerant kinds include the hybrids of these species, such as the Bellingham hybrids, the Trumpet hybrids, and the Orientals.

Feeling the Heat

Looking at an atlas and plotting the homelands of the wild lilies would suggest that, while a fair sprinkling live in the cooler latitudes of the northern hemisphere, a lot of the species come from places in America and in Asia where they might be expected to feel the heat on their backs. One might begin to worry about hardiness zones and start revising geography long forgotten. For gardeners in the temperate regions where cold wet winters are usual and the summers may, or may not, be marked by periods of unbroken warm sunshine, a preoccupation with the vagaries of the weather is the constant background to all domestic and gardening planning. Dare we have a barbeque party on Tuesday week?

L. michauxii is the Carolina lily, the more southern part of the *L. superbum* complex, reaching from southern Virginia through North and South Carolina into Florida and heading for the Tropic of Cancer. In India the trumpet kind, *L. neilgherrense*, is found sometimes within 10° of the equator, which makes it the most southerly of all lilies. The species *L. philippinense* and *L. formosanum* both indicate exotic spots that make one think of the pleasures of long cool drinks and the blessings of air conditioning. But looking casually at maps can be deceptive unless one studies the matter more closely. *L. neilgherrense* comes from hills 6,000–8,500ft (1,800–2,500m) high, *L. philippinense* comes from a latitude of around 18° but belongs to the mountains of the north islands, *L. formosanum*, from Taiwan (Formosa), is found from sea level up to 12,000ft (3,500m). Altitude affects the hardiness rating of the plants, the small forms of *L. formosanum* from higher up the mountains, over 5,000ft (1,500m), are really quite hardy, and even some of the larger ones from the lower slopes can be surprisingly resilient. It is often worth trying out a few bulbs of such types just to see whether they may confound expectation and flourish.

The growth of all lilies is triggered primarily by warmth. When the soil warms up in spring the bulbs respond quickly and send out rapidly extending stems. Bulbs of most types planted in pots and kept in the greenhouse with a temperature of 60°F (16°C) will come into rapid growth. In very few days the buds are bursting through the surface, athletes off their starting blocks on their way to flowering, a race that they will complete in a mere fourteen weeks.

Naturalized Lilies

The idea of naturalizing daffodils is something that comes easily to mind, but naturalizing lilies at first seems rather an up-market bit of extravagance. Second thoughts will show that this is not necessarily so. All that is needed is a lily that is able to grow happily for years with no fussing in grass, in woodland, between shrubs. Leading contenders are the stronger American species, *L. pardalinum* and its like, the *L. martagon* clan in its various forms, *L. hansonii*, all the fine hybrids between these two species, and tough types like *L. pyrenaicum*. Finally, any lily particularly suited to the soil and conditions of your garden is a prime candidate. So, it may well be that, while most Asiatic hybrids would look much too dressed-up in their party gear, the North hybrids, with their pendent pastel flowers, could look splendid, given soil that is well endowed with gritty humus, has good drainage, and is on the acid side of neutral. Lily buffs fight shy of the tiger lily, *L. lancifolium*, because it is a notorious carrier of virus infection. However, it can provide a late burst of colour if sited well away from other lilies and can give reliable service for years.

While these hardy, naturalizing types will cope well over the years with most sites, it would certainly be prudent and only fair to give some thought to the soil and site when planting them in their permanent homes. This will mean thoroughly digging over the planting site, incorporating generous amounts of humus at least into the top spit, and doing what may be possible to ensure good drainage. Soakaway channels or a line of land drains to lower ground may be needed on sites with serious problems of excess moisture. Finding a site that is naturally drained is of course the best answer.

The physical structure of the soil is part of the equation that will give you the answer to adequate carrying away of water, but the surrounding vegetation will also be an important factor. Thus the trees and shrubs of light woodland will help by the extensive root systems they build in the soil, by the transpiration of water through their leaves, by natural shelter, and by the changing structure of the soil they establish through the accumulation of years of fallen leaves. Once planted, our naturalizing lilies are going to be left to get on with their own life while we fuss around the more demanding plants, cut the grass, and clip the hedge.

Beds and Borders

Lilies are excellent in the mixed border. They give drama and class to the whole. The height of many would make them a focal point even should their colours not immediately beckon. In truth they are better in mixed company than by themselves. Surrounding plants provide shade for their roots that they appreciate.

Asiatics are robust growers, quick to increase in reasonable conditions, and so in need of lifting and dividing every two or three years. Many species may be planted and left to proceed with their lives until they eventually get overcrowded and it becomes an obvious mercy some few weeks after blooming to divide up the competing bulbs to give them more room and fresh soil. Stands of Martagons or Americans may well be left alone forever to bloom each summer. One of the newer American

hybrids – 'Cherrywood', for example – could look exceptionally stylish between shrubs, but then the old Martagon hybrid 'Marhan', bred last century, also has plenty of vigour and is certainly a beautiful flower.

Obtaining Bulbs

Joe's hardware store will have lilies at any time after the plastic Christmas trees have been put away and before big discounts are being given on summer garden furniture. Chain stores are in on the act. Lilies are business. Garden centres and nurseries will have more and are increasingly offering bulbs from the end of the summer. Kinds on offer are the easy-to-propagate, easy-to-grow kinds, Asiatics and Trumpets. Bulb growers and traders producing catalogues will have lilies featured. A few growers specialize in lilies, some with a wide range, some with a limited number of interesting kinds. Such growers are worth seeking out.

There are lilies that are not grown extensively by the trade because they are awkward to lift and package. Some are even awkward to grow. How does one obtain these? The answer is to peruse the seed catalogues of enterprising firms who may well be listing a surprising number of equally surprising kinds. Many grow quickly from seed. A second answer to the query is to join a specialist lily organization and take part in the activities of like-minded enthusiasts who will be happy to exchange or give away surplus bulbs of a wide range of kinds. Here is the ideal; one's social life is enhanced, one's education is widened, and sources of otherwise unobtainable kinds are revealed.

Planting

Lilies need good drainage and they like an open gritty soil with plenty of humus. It makes sense, therefore to dig deeply and do what lies in one's power to provide such a rooting medium.

Bulbs may be planted at various times. Ideally, in one's own garden or when acquiring bulbs from friends, it may be possible to do this some three or four weeks after blooming. So the bulbs of most types may be in their new sites with well-established root runs before winter cold and wet brings activity to a near-dormant state and provides

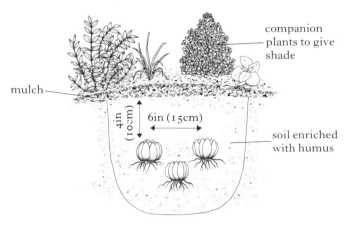

companion plants to give shade

mulch

4in (10cm)

6in (15cm)

soil enriched with humus

Planting lilies outdoors

the chance for bacteria and pests to attack. From commercial sources it is sometimes possible to obtain early autumn delivery. This is fine – the soil is still warm and bulbs will arrive with some live roots attached. But most bulb sellers send out their lilies at the end of winter or in early spring. These bulbs may have spent some weeks or months in a cold store before they arrive at your door. They will be none the worse for this.

If the weather is not so cold and the ground not so sodden that it makes the task almost unthinkable, then they may be planted out. If conditions do not permit this, the bulbs can be stored for a few weeks in a cool spot in peat that is damp but not wet. With better weather, and the daffodils shooting, we can sally forth and plant. Alternatively, if these better weather conditions seem too far off, the bulbs can be planted up in pots and then the growing potful planted out later.

Early spring planting has a lot in its favour. Older literature would advise autumn planting, and from the above one perhaps can see the sense of this advice, but times past were addressing slightly different problems with different resources. The lilies then being grown were heavily dominated by the species, and the written suggestions were being addressed to people who would order their lilies, expect delivery when it suited them, and have the head gardener arrange for some of the undergardeners to deal with the bulbs. Times have changed. Storing bulbs in cold stores was not a technique readily available to traders in the past. Our bulbs come plump and ready for action. Their roots are quickly extruded, the food-packed scales provide the boost to launch root and stem activity. The plants grow away without check, provided there is no unusual occurrence like a late hard frost. Any lily susceptible to frost would be damaged on such a rare occasion.

Many lilies produce roots from their stems below the soil surface and therefore it makes sense to allow some depth of soil for the bulbs to take advantage of this propensity. Even non-stem rooters will benefit from sensibly deep planting, which helps to keep the bulbs cool and to anchor the stem in the soil. Most normal-sized bulbs will need at least 4in (10cm) of soil over their tops and would be better for 6in (15cm) at least in all but the heaviest of soils. In difficult, heavy soils the strategy should be to plant just a little less deeply and then to build up the soil level over the bulbs above that of the surrounding ground. Mulches will be a very big help. Small bulbs, such as those of *L. pumilum*, *L. concolor*, or some of the little nomocharis-like types may be less deeply plunged but will be still quite deep in proportion to their size.

Space allowance for lilies will depend on how long it is envisaged that they will stay in the site, how conscientious they are about increasing, and how large the plants are. In the garden, plan a few bold groups of lilies; they are far more effective than many scattered singletons. Single bulbs may be purchased of expensive kinds but if possible it is much more effective to plant three, five, ten, or twenty of a kind. Most single bulbs can be quickly propagated by scales. Within a group a minimum of 6in (15cm) between bulbs would seem prudent. Kinds to be left for many years, such as some American species, *L. martagon*, or their hybrids should be given plenty of room so that they may increase without getting too crowded. Some 12in (30cm) or more would not be too generous.

Feeding

When in full growth lilies drink deeply and will take plenty of feed, but they are not plants for force-feeding. There is no need to buy large amounts of artificial foodstuffs. If we can manage with the nutrients in the soil, generously augmented by doses of well-made compost, then this is the ideal. However, such advice does not entirely preclude the use of additives. Fertilizers with a nitrogen, phosphorus, potassium (NPK) balance of 5.10.10 or 5.10.5 may be usefully applied before the shoots appear in the spring, at the rate of 2–3oz per sq. yard (70–100g per m²). The fertilizer should just be tickled into the surface soil. A second, lighter, application may be given later in the season. Care should be taken that the raw fertilizer does not touch stem or leaf.

Fertilizer high in nitrogen should be avoided, this element tending to encourage leaf and stem growth. Tomato fertilizers, being rich in potash, are often useful and can be used as liquid feeds.

Lilies, like all bulbs, enjoy potash; as sulphate of potash or the dry ashes from a wood-burning stove, this may be carefully sprinkled around plants and worked into the top inch or top couple of centimetres of the soil. Do not splash it around too freely, especially in the presence of rhododendrons, as it is alkaline and will provoke an untoward reaction. Phosphorus promotes healthy root action.

Mulching

Mulches around the lilies give food, they conserve moisture, they keep the roots cool, they should inhibit weed growth, they get incorporated into the structure of the soil, and they obviate the need to hoe around the plants, an operation fraught with the probability, if not certainty, that damage will be done to the exploring roots sent out by the stems. Mulches are a very good thing.

Keeping the plants free of weed will help to provide less shelter and encouragement for slugs and similar creepy nasties.

Making the Most of Lilies

Lilies are gregarious – they look happier in company. Visually it is much more effective to grow only a few kinds, and to plant them in bold groups, than to try to have a bulb or so of as many kinds as possible. Yellows, gold, and oranges are bright extrovert carnival colours that come halfway down the garden to greet you. Perhaps they need planting with some discretion. We need such brightness, but it may well be the more effective if restricted to one or two focal points. Few other flowers can live close to a group of 'Enchantment' – the colour dominates its surroundings. Best to accompany it by the neutral but attractive silvery-leaved *Senecio* 'Sunshine' and with ferns than attempt a colour scheme that could shout to the rooftops. The red-flowered kinds, still all bright and cheerful, manage this without quite such aggressive individuality. Surrounding plants and flowers can make their contribution. Altogether easier are the pale creams and pinks of Asiatics such as 'Mont Blanc', 'Sterling Star', and 'Rosita'. The North hybrids and the Martagons are dramatic; they have more pastel colours and are easier to associate with all types of plants and flowers.

Recommended Lilies

Gardeners are inveterate list makers – of seeds, of desirable plants, of affordable plants; in the winter, of things to do in the spring and summer; in the spring and summer, of things to do in the winter. Opposite are some more. Treat them only as suggestions.

Pot and Container Culture

Bulbs placed in compost in a pot and kept at a temperature of 60°F (15°C) will break through the surface in a few days and will be blooming in fourteen weeks. Lilies are the easiest of bulbs to grow in containers. Species that resent disturbance, such as *L. martagon*, or ones that have an inbuilt dislike of cultivation may well prove tricky, but even these may be a whole lot easier when grown under controlled conditions in containers, where they can at least be kept dryish in the winter, so avoiding one common difficulty. Hybrid lilies grow as if especially bred for the purpose of container growing. The only problem with Trumpet kinds is their height – the Pink Perfections of the hybrid world can be a considerable load for a pot.

Later-blooming *L. speciosum* and *L. auratum* kinds are brought forward to open earlier by extra warmth and are happy in containers, where the compost may be kept safely free of lime. The readily available modern Asiatic hybrids are the easiest lilies of all for pot growing. They grow quickly and healthily and are not too tall to manage easily. Most will reach about 30in (75cm) high and are sturdy. One or two are shorter and so are even more tailor-made for pots. 'Harmony' and 'Bingo' will normally grow only to some 18in

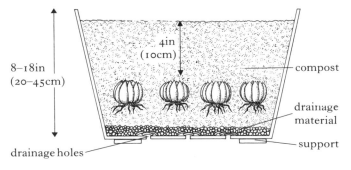

Planting lilies in a container

For heavy soils
L. brownii
L. chalcedonicum
L. hansonii
L. humboldtii
L. martagon
L. pardalinum
L. parryi
L. tsingtauense
together with hybrids of these.

For ease of growing

'African Queen'	'Rosita'
'Black Dragon'	'Sunray'
'Discovery'	*L. davidii*
'Enchantment'	*L. formosanum*
'Festival'	*L. henryi*
Golden Splendour	*L. lancifolium*
'Green Dragon'	*L. martagon*
'Mont Blanc'	*L. regale*
Pink Perfection	*L. speciosum*

For scent
L. auratum
L. candidum
L. cernuum
L. formosanum
L. lankogense
L. monadelphum
L. pumilum
L. regale
L. speciosum
L. superbum
L. washingtonianum
plus hybrids of these and all Trumpet types.

For succession of flower
L. pyrenaicum (late spring, early summer)
L. pumilum (early summer)
Asiatic hybrids (early to mid-summer)
L. martagon and hybrids (early to mid-summer)
L. regale (mid- to late summer)
Golden Splendour (mid- to late summer)
Trumpet hybrids (mid- to late summer)
L. pardalinum (mid- to late summer)
L. lancifolium (late summer, early autumn)
L. auratum (late summer, early autumn)
L. speciosum (late summer, early autumn)
L. formosanum (early autumn)

(45cm) or so. 'Harmony', in a very pleasing soft apricot, is a particularly early kind and in a container it will flower at the end of the winter or in very early spring.

The routine of growing is simplicity itself. Containers need drainage. The pots need to be large enough to allow at least 4in (10cm) of compost over the tops of the bulbs. Though single bulbs will grow easily in small pots – as small as 5in (13cm) for one bulb – it is much easier to keep the bulbs moist, at a steady temperature, and anchored if they are grown in larger ones. Three Asiatics or Orientals can be grown in an 8in (20cm) pot. A single, larger, Trumpet lily will need the same space. A 10in (25cm) pot will take five smaller types or three large Trumpets.

Composts sold for ericaceous plants will suit all lilies. Made-up composts of equal parts of leaf mould, loam, and rough sand or grit work well. If there is any variation in the proportions, the humus content can be enlarged it certainly should not be depleted. Well-rotted, crumbly compost may take the place of leaf mould. If neither of these is available one will have to use peat to provide humus content and water-retaining ability, but this will have no nutritional value and then it will be more important to incorporate some artificial feed. A sprinkling of a proprietary mix suitable for tomatoes or potatoes is excellent.

Some compost is placed in the pot or container, the bulb or bulbs added, and the pots filled to half an inch or a centimetre or so of the top. There should be at least 4in (10cm) over the noses.

As lilies in pots kept in the warm may be in bloom in about three months it is an easy matter to arrange a succession of bloom from late winter through until the autumn by planting bulbs in a succession and employing kinds that bloom naturally at differing times. Bulbs not needed for immediate planting can be kept for a while in the winter or very early spring in a cool spot lying in damp peat. Later, when the temperature is higher, the bulbs may be inclined to shoot, regardless of the fact that they are not properly planted. Then they may be kept dormant by being held for a few weeks in the domestic refrigerator.

An unheated greenhouse or a conservatory is ideal for potted bulbs. The temperature will be more variable and the fourteen weeks to flowering will be extended a little, but the plants will develop beautifully and all can be enjoyed without any need to fear late frosts, or animal pests.

The potfuls can be enjoyed where they are growing or, being transportable, taken to a living room or placed out on the patio. They could be stationed at some strategic position in the garden. This makes the container in which they are growing of greater importance. The range of earthenware and plastic planters is now so wide as to be almost confusing. There is no doubt that people will prefer the traditional earthenware over the plastic offerings, but some of the latter are now very much more pleasing and may be less expensive. A half tub will maintain a good reservoir of moisture and nutrients in a bulk of compost that will be less liable to major fluctuations of root temperatures, but will be big enough to allow other plants to be grown alongside the lilies, perhaps foliage kinds that will enhance the whole picture.

Cut Flowers

Some, even many, gardeners are careful, not to say mean, with their blooming lilies. The flowers belong to the garden and only occasionally will stems be cut to bring inside. It is a miserly attitude that I have myself. Cutting the lily means depriving it of some of its strength. Of course one does not need to take the whole stem and I know well enough that if only half the stem is taken the plant will not really feel the loss very much. I just like to see them in the garden. It is not one of life's most difficult problems. Bulbs can be quickly increased; a number of bulbs can be planted out in the kitchen garden or in some place not too important to the whole garden design. Here everything is fair game. Certainly a room may be brought to life with a few stems.

Flower arranging can be as simple or as involved as you wish. Half a day may be spent on an arrangement, or a single stem dropped into a straight-sided vase. The lily has already arranged itself, the flowers are disposed in an attractive manner, it is the flower for the non-arranger. A stem, or maybe three, of a lily alone or with a little foliage such as a fern will look just right. *L. speciosum* as a single stem will scent a room. Lilies charm all the senses.

Exhibiting

You may be persuaded that it would be fun to enter the local summer flower show. There is a class for lilies or bulbous plants. What one needs is a stem or stems with two or three fully open fresh flowers and other buds to come. There should be no question of any flowers showing signs of old age. Flowers are best cut the evening before the show and left overnight in water. This they will take up and become much harder, sometimes surprisingly more firm than when taken from the garden. The greatest problem in transporting the lily stems to the show is to ensure that the bright pollen does not fall and besmirch the petals. It is sticky and almost impossible to get off. It is prudent therefore, before moving the stem at all, to surround the anthers with tissue held gently with a rubber band or to enclose them in a small plastic bag. The tissue or bag can be carefully removed when the stem has been transported and finally arranged in its vase. It is probably the last job before the judges come round. Normally an exhibited lily will be shown to be fully in character, upright, with no diseases or damage showing, firmly anchored in its vase, and neatly labelled.

5

PESTS AND DISEASES

All living things have their troubles. Lilies are not excessively burdened, though sometimes writers seem to dwell at such length on the various vicissitudes that may befall the plants that they may deter the intending cultivator. The worst pest could be the lily beetle. In Britain this is confined to certain southern counties. The worst disease problem is likely to be an attack by virus.

Diseases

Virus Diseases

There are several virus diseases that will attack lilies; some are kinds that may be present in other neighbouring plants, such as tulips, so it is wise to keep these plants well away from lilies. The diagnosis of disease can sometimes be a problem. One particular virus disease may affect different lilies in completely different ways. *L. formosanum* reacts so quickly and dramatically to virus – its leaves, stems and flowers become streaked and distorted – that it is sometimes used as an indicator plant for the presence of disease. Other species may get infected and carry on living for ages, managing a creditable performance in the garden. But of course such infected stock is a constant threat to all lilies.

There is no garden cure for virus. Infected bulbs should be destroyed, or, if the bulbs are very important, they must be kept in as strict a quarantine as possible until clean replacements are to hand. In the laboratory the meristem of a bulb may be cleared of virus and new tissue grown on to provide the basis for fresh, clean stock. Virus is not carried by seed, so new stock of a species can be raised and the parent bulbs safely destroyed. It is often difficult immediately to spot virus infection in lilies bred from more virus-tolerant species such as *L. lancifolium*, *L. davidii*, and *L. bulbiferum*.

Lily mottle virus causes the leaves to become streaked and mottled. The plant is weakened until eventually it dies. It is the same virus that causes the striping of broken tulips.

Cucumber mosaic virus reduces such species as *L. formosanum* to twisted wrecks. More resistant lilies show mottling or streaking of their leaves with paler, sometimes almost yellow, discoloration. Leaves and flowers can become twisted. *L. lancifolium* is a prime suspect as a carrier for this virus, the symptoms being less obvious in its leaves than in other lilies. All infected bulbs should be burnt.

Lily symptomless virus is a particularly troublesome disease. Plants continue to grow but show no obvious signs of infection, merely not doing as well as they ought. They slowly lose ground and, sooner or later, depending on the variety, will peter out.

Fungal Diseases

Botrytis usually first attacks the lower leaves, these become wasted, browned, and shriveled up. The spores of *Botrytis elliptica* produce on the leaves dark red or brown spots that spread and join to produce a scorched appearance. If not checked the trouble can proceed up the stem, the dead leaves dropping and leaving just a gaunt flagpole with perhaps a few green leaves at the masthead. All diseased tissue should be burned to prevent the wind-borne spores spreading infection. Botrytis rarely kills the bulb, but it can obviously severely weaken it; very bad attacks can attack the bulb itself. The fungus is encouraged by a poor circulation of air and is worst in wet, still, humid conditions. A cold wet spring is a danger time. A twenty-four-hour soak in Benlate prior to planting is a sensible bit of hygiene. Growing plants sprayed at ten-day intervals with Bordeaux mixture, Benlate, or Captan until flower buds are fully formed will be kept safe from infection. Botrytis is not normally a serious problem, given normal good cultivation.

Basal rot is caused by the fungus *Fusarium oxysporum*, which attacks various bulbous and other plants. It will normally attack a bulb where the scales join the base plate. Any bulb bases that appear damaged when planting should have their affected parts cut away and the cleaned bulbs soaked in fungicide before being planted in a position where they have healthy rooting conditions and good drainage. Keep clear of positions where this fungus has been operating, as the soil will be infected.

Sometimes you may find plants in which the leaves have taken on a choleric purple appearance. This is likely to indicate that all is far from being well at bulb level. The plant should be lifted, and any rotten roots and scales removed, then dipped in fungicide, and replanted in a healthy situation.

If leaves take on a sad, yellowish complexion, it may be that they are suffering from an excess of lime, something that many lilies dislike. Lime in the soil can be best counteracted by generous amounts of peat, leaf mould, and compost, all of which will help to bring the pH level away from the alkaline to the acid side. Sulphur and sulphate of ammonia will help. However all these additives are part of a long-term strategy. In the short term the best bet is to spray with a chelated iron compound.

Pests

These come in various shapes and sizes. Rabbits will nibble shoots when there is nothing better on offer, and where they are a regular garden pest it is best to try to physically protect groups of lilies.

This may be done by encircling each group with a firmly anchored ring of chicken-wire standing at least 2ft (60cm), and preferably 30in (75cm), high. While this may look unsightly at first, surrounding vegetation can quickly mask it.

Mice, rats, and squirrels have been known to be a nuisance on occasions. You will take your usual choice of combative action.

Slugs
These are one of the major problems. They will be at their underground worst when the bulbs are just getting nicely under way; they can eat into the shoots badly enough to cause them to break and the bulb to have an almost wasted year. Clean cultivation and normal anti-slug precautions should keep this menace under control.

Aphids
These insects suck nourishment from the plant tissue. The disfigurement they cause is bad enough, but they also carry virus diseases from plant to plant. Spraying with a systemic insecticide will kill them.

Lily Beetle
The handsome scarlet lily beetle, which attacks lily foliage, can be picked off and destroyed, but its dirty cream larvae, which also attack the leaves, are harder to gather up and dispatch. Both mature beetles and larvae, however are powerless against one of the normal pesticide sprays. Early action is desirable, the beetles are exceedingly voracious and they seem to prefer the most expensive lilies. Mature larvae stay in the top soil for the winter; it could be that when any lilies are lifted they should be replanted in fresh locations some distance away.

Eelworms
These nematodes, invisible to normal sight, can attack lilies. They can be killed by hot-water-treatment, one hour at 44°C (111°F). This will also kill bulb mite, a pest that is usually serious only in very warm areas.

Enchantment

Most famous of lily hybrids, 'Enchantment' has, since its introduction in 1947, been grown in countless millions. Its ease of culture, robust nature, and excellent flower form and colour have meant that it has held its own against the competition of many newer cultivars–many of them with 'Enchantment' blood in them. It has such an entrenched position in the trade that new virus-free stock is regularly propagated.

Casablanca
This large-flowered Oriental hybrid (right) has proved itself one of the best of a series of cultivars – now being widely grown. All-round plant health is excellent and the stem is strong and able to cope with a heavy flower load.

Lilium speciosum rubrum
Thought by many fanciers to
be the loveliest of the species
lilies, the flower form, colour,
and texture and the gorgeous
perfume of *Lilium speciosum
rubrum* (right) combine to
ensure its popularity. Its leaves
are gracefully held on the
stalks and the distinctive,
large, widely spaced pendent
flowers are of great beauty. It
is a lime hater.

Festival
Introduced in 1980, but of
unknown parentage, 'Festival'
(left) is one of the strongest-
growing Asiatics. With its
mahogany-purple stems and
strong, dark leaves, it always
looks the picture of health. Its
robust nature is reflected also
in the freedom with which it
produces masses of plump
bulbils in the leaf axils.

35

Montreaux
Since the introduction of the rather gaudy Mid-Century hybrids – exemplified by such lilies as 'Enchantment' and 'Destiny' – there has been a tendency to breed paler, more subtly coloured hybrids. 'Montreaux' (left) is one of the best of these, but there are many others, some of which have had only a fairly short commercial life – not because of any deficiency in health or beauty but simply through the press of numbers of fine new Asiatics.

Olivia
Like all the Oriental hybrids, 'Olivia' (above) grows beautifully in pots or tubs or other containers, and in these cossetted conditions it is easy to provide the lime-free diet it needs. It is – again like all its Oriental fellows – a later flowerer than the Asiatics. These Asiatics will bear the closest examination so that we can not only enjoy the colouring but also appreciate the texture and luxuriate in the intoxicating perfume.

Apeldoorn
A clean, strong growth pattern of shining leaves and stems has helped to ensure that 'Apeldoorn' (above) still maintains its popularity after a quarter century in commerce – it was introduced in 1965. It was bred from *Lilium davidii* crossed with a very old Hollandicum hybrid, 'Erect', and is living proof that kinds close to the species can have quite outstanding vigour and character.

Lilium martagon
This, the world's most widely
distributed lily species,
displays a very unfussy
attitude to soil and conditions
– it has on many occasions
escaped the confines of the
garden and successfully
established itself in meadows
and light woodland. Part of
this adaptability is a complete
indifference to the presence of
lime in the soil.

'Tamara
Introduced in 1979, 'Tamara' is one of the upward-facing Asiatics that are so useful in borders, in pots, or as cut flowers. It bears a number of medium-sized flowers in well-spaced heads.

39

Lilium martagon album
In some areas of its natural
distribution in eastern Europe
Lilium martagon has produced
white forms without human
intervention. Other white
forms have arisen in
cultivation from stock raised
from seed. Most of these *L. m.
album* forms (above, left and
right) have flowers that are in
colour a uniform ivory-white.
In the garden these white lilies
are very effective among the
standard mauve-pinks of the
species lilies – the two colours
highlight one another. There
are some rarer albinos with a
light peppering of dark dots
towards the flower centres.

Lilium henryi
Lilium henryi (right), is
perhaps the most useful of
lilies, easy to grow in a wide
range of temperate regions. It
is a strong plant, far more
persistent as a bulb than most
species – which tend to rely
more on seed to perpetuate
themselves. *Lilium henryi*,
although it does grow well
from seed, has bulbs that will
persist for decades even in
difficult situations. To give the
best results, it welcomes deep,
well-drained soil, but it is
indifferent to the presence or
absence of lime. Flowers hold
their colours best in some
shade – strong sun bleaches
them.

Lilium candidum
The madonna lily has been a much-loved plant for many centuries; it has probably had a longer association with man than any other lily – although it was adopted into Christian symbolism its culture long predates Christianity. It is also one of the few plants still grown today in the flower garden that is listed in the earliest-known English treatise on gardening, *The Feate of Gardening*, written in about 1400.

Lilium auratum

This magnificent species, which grows wild on Japanese mountainsides, in poor soils derived from volcanic ash, has been a cynosure in gardens ever since it has been in cultivation. Its stems can have many blooms, each 10in (25cm) across. It falls an easy prey to viruses and so ideally should be grown where it can avoid the attentions of sap-sucking insects.

Lilium regale
There is little new left to say
about this wonderful species
lily (above). It can be
recommended wholeheartedly
to a newcomer to lily growing,
but is also one that no veteran
would want to be without. It is
worth growing, apart from its
beauty, for its intoxicating
perfume. It should be planted
in a sunny position, but it is
not fussy as to soil and it is
very quick to bloom from
plants raised from seed.

Lilium concolor
Lilium concolor (right) is a
delightful small species that
blooms from a tiny bulb and
looks most dainty and bright.
Only about 1ft–2ft 6in
(30–75cm) high, it makes a
delightful pot lily. Although
difficult to cross-fertilize, it is
now entering the breeding of
some Asiatic strains. Hybrids
are stronger and longer-lived.

Lilium bulbiferum croceum

This, the orange lily (right), is the form that usually represents in cultivation the European species *Lilium bulbiferum*. It is one of the most important founder species in the breeding of many Asiatic hybrids, to which it brings the benefits of vigour, early flowering, and good foliage.

Diplomat

'Diplomat' (below) is a strong, mid-season Asiatic bred from an 'Orange Light' seedling crossed with 'Connecticut King' and introduced in 1979. It is one of the many hybrids that are showing an increased tolerance to a wide range of soil conditions and so are valuable for the home gardener.

Brushmark

This is the best known of a number of hybrids that sport a distinctive patch of contrasted colour on each petal. In 'Brushmark' in particular, this looks as though it has been added by a painter.

Lilium pardalinum

For many gardens this, the leopard lily (left), typifies the American group of wild lilies. It is a hardy, easily grown lily that makes spectacular rhizomatous bulb growth – a piece with one bud may manage in a single season to make up to five new buds. In the garden it is best suited by moist but well-drained soil.

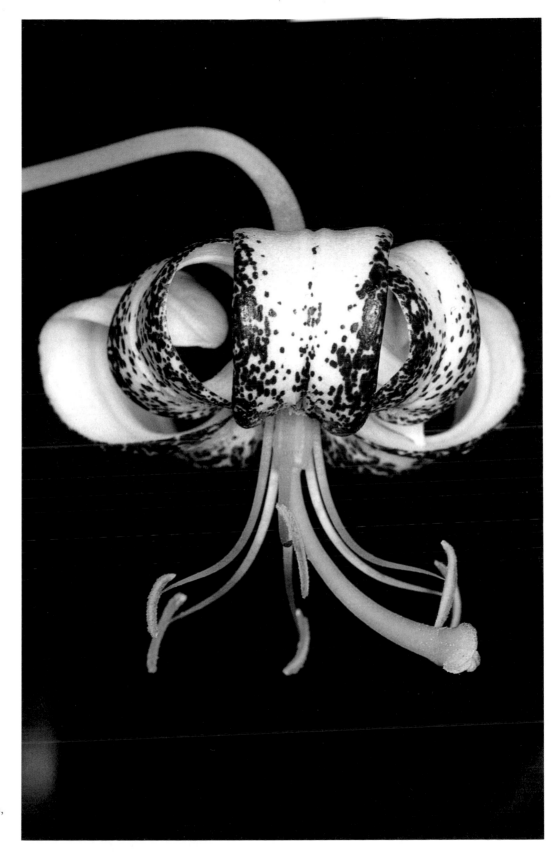

Lilium duchartrei

This lovely species lily from Asia (right) is somewhat variable in height, but rather less so in flower size and form. It is nomadic, in the sense that bulbs send out stems that meander underground, forming new bulbs at intervals, before turning up into the daylight.

Lilium pumilum

Still often listed as *Lilium tenuifolium*, this species (left) has small bulbs that, when not much bigger than marbles, will surge into rapid spring growth and produce several nodding blooms on a single wiry stem. Grown in pots it may be brought into bloom in April or May. Heavy seeding can imperil the life of the bulbs, but seed grows quickly into flowering bulbs.

Lilium lancifolium
The tiger lily (above), known for ages as *Lilium tigrinum*, now exists under this revised name. It is a late summer flowerer of abundant vigour – it can quickly form impressive stands by bulb division or by the growing on of the numerous bulbils that form in the leaf axils. There are both diploid and triploid forms, most of the garden sorts being triploids.

Lilium parryi
This (above), is one of the more distinctive of the North American species. It can achieve quite extraordinary feats of blossoming, carrying sometimes more than two dozen outward-facing flowers on stems that may be up to 6ft (1.8m) high. Growth is rapid after emergence. Enjoying moisture when active, dormant bulbs are best kept dryish.

Lilium rubellum

This Japanese species is a most refined and graceful small lily that reaches a height of 1ft–1ft 6in (30–75cm). It is stem rooting and in deep, cool, humus-rich, lime-free soil in partial shade it may exist happily for a number of seasons, but its reputation is as a lily that it is not easy to grow well.

Sutton Court
Raised in 1925, 'Sutton Court' is named after the house near the city of Hereford in central England where its raisers, Mr and Mrs R. O. Backhouse, lived. Some still grow wild in the garden there. These *L. martagon* hybrids are the most persistent of lilies.

Lilium superbum
Although it can sometimes make itself at home in other continents, *Lilium superbum* (left) is an American species – and one of the finest. Its stems can sometimes reach a height of 8ft (2.4m); they carry many well-spaced blooms. Although not difficult to grow well, it will not tolerate lime.

Little Gem
'Little Gem' (right) is a selected clone from the form *Lilium auratum platyphyllum*, which is more resistant to disease than the type species, the golden-rayed lily of Japan. Because 'Little Gem' remains dwarf, it is particularly useful for growing in pots.

Lilium formosanum pricei
Lilium formosanum is a species of the Trumpet group that is usually considered to be rather tender. The dwarf form, *L. f. pricei* (left), derived from seed collected higher up the mountainsides than that of the type, is more hardy, but is somewhat variable.

Lilium pyrenaicum rubrum
Lilium pyrenaicum is the earliest lily to bloom outside. It is hardy – in Britain it has escaped from gardens to grow wild in Devon hedgerows. In warm temperate gardens it is a very easy and long-lived lily, but it may sulk when first planted, not appearing above the surface at all during the first year. Its flowers are normally bright yellow, but shown here is *L. p. rubrum* (right), the much rarer orange-red form.

Pink Tiger und Sunray
These two varieties (left) make
here a cheerfully contrasted
pair, but usually 'Pink Tiger'
will bloom after 'Sunray',
whose flowers come in early
summer. 'Pink Tiger' is bred
from a *Lilium lancifolium*
hybrid crossed with
'Discovery'; for 'Sunray' see
also page 91. Both are good
garden plants and excellent in
pots.

Marhan
This outstanding variety
(right) is still one of the best of
all garden hybrids. It was bred
from *Lilium martagon album*
with *L. hansonii*, and so is one
of the group of such hybrids
known collectively as
L. × dalhansonii. 'Marhan' is a
strong plant, indifferent to
lime, and capable of building
up into a stand of lilies that
will last for many decades.

Duet

This fine Asiatic cultivar (left) has softer colour tones than the more commonly grown variety 'Connecticut King' (shown on page 64), and is perhaps for this reason the more appealing in garden schemes. It also differs from 'Connecticut King' in having a light scattering of spots. Blooming in June and July, it is a very sturdy plant some 30in (90cm) high.

Mont Blanc

This sturdy Asiatic (above), introduced in 1978, is a seedling from the well-known 'Yellow Blaze' (above right), which was itself from 'Nutmegger' × *Lilium wilsonii flavium*. 'Mont Blanc' is still used extensively in the cut-flower trade as well as being grown as a garden and pot plant. It gives very pleasing seedlings.

Yellow Blaze

This (above) is one of the earlier of the hybrids produced by the Stone and Payne partnership that virtually cornered the market in yellow Asiatics, producing the ubiquitous 'Connecticut King' (see page 64) and varieties without spots. 'Yellow Blaze' introduced in 1965, remains an excellent pot plant for the patio as well as a desirable garden and cut flower.

Stargazer

'Stargazer', introduced in 1975, has proved to be the most useful of the many Oriental hybrids. It blooms from a very small bulb, grows easily, and responds readily to pot culture and to forcing; its stems are very strong and not too tall. All this adds up to just what is needed both in a cut flower and in a garden plant.

Jetfire

From a *Lilium × hollandicum* cultivar crossed with 'Connecticut King', 'Jetfire' (opposite below), which dates from 1971, has proved a popular garden variety, not least because its mixed colouring makes a pleasing contrast to many other commonly grown lilies. It is an altogether excellent, strong plant, whose bulbs increase quickly by division.

Golden Splendour

It is a measure of the thoroughness of the work done by the de Graaff team that this series (above left), a selection from the original Golden Clarion strain, still, after more than thirty years, contains the most widely grown varieties of golden Trumpet lilies. The genetic background of the Golden Splendour lilies is the original interbreeding of *Lilium henryi* with Trumpets such as *L. sargentiae* and *L. leucantheum*; it is the *L. henryi* input that helps to make these strong plants so persistent.

Lilium speciosum album

The white forms of the glorious scented Japanese species *Lilium speciosum* are among the loveliest of lilies – and, indeed, of all garden flowers. *L. s. album* (above) needs lime-free, humus-rich soil and plenty of moisture when in growth. Its natural late summer or autumn flowering period can be brought forward by pot culture under glass. It will perfume the greenhouse or a single stem brought inside will scent a room.

Connecticut King
Undoubtedly the most successful lily bred by the American partnership of Stone and Payne, 'Connecticut King' (left) is the only cultivar that even remotely approaches the megastar success of 'Enchantment'. Introduced in 1967, it is a wonderful commercial plant and a stalwart garden variety.

Silver Swan
One of a series of newer hybrids of sparkling, pristine perfection, 'Silver Swan' (right) grows well outside as well as in pots. It belies its exotic appearance by proving to be a good sturdy garden plant.

Concorde
'Concorde' (left) is a beautiful upward-facing Asiatic hybrid. Its parentage is a yellow Connecticut hybrid pollinated by the wide-flowered *Lilium dauricum*. 'Concorde' is a very robust selection, from the 'Sundrop' grex bred 1972.

Citronella
This (above) is a strain, introduced by Jan de Graaff in 1958, not a variety, so there is some variability from plant to plant – the number of flowers, their size, and the degree of spotting being the characteristics most likely to differ.

Pink Perfection
Like Citronella, this is a strain, not a single variety. Pink Perfection can reach an impressive size – sometimes as much as 7ft (2m) high. Early Pink Perfections included pale pink kinds, but nowadays bulbs on offer are likely to be clones of dark-toned plants.

Bright Star

'Bright Star' (left) is one of the Sunburst strain of Aurelian hybrids bred by de Graaff. It has much of the *Lilium henryi* habit of growth and is certainly the most successful representative of this wide-flowered strain – few others of which are now available.

Lilium chalcedonicum

Virtually all European species have become extinct, rare, or threatened in the wild and *Lilium chalcedonicum* (right), once a common garden plant, is now, sadly, rare in cultivation too. Its colour is splendid, and much enhanced by its high-gloss finish.

Lilium leichtlinii
This pleasing Asian species (right) has been marketed at various times in the form of selections originally made in the wild. *Lilium leichtlinii maximowiczii*, a red-flowered kind, has been the commoner form in cultivation.

Escapade
One of the rather newer Asiatic hybrids, and standing out from that crowd of richly coloured varieties as one of the very best, 'Escapade' (right) has large, wide heads of durable, unfading flowers. In addition, the stems are very firm and the foliage dark and healthy.

Lilium taliense

Lilium taliense (right) is a beautiful relative of *Lilium duchartrei* that was first introduced into cultivation in the mid-1930s but proved to be by no means easy to keep. It is variable, with some clones producing new bulbs on wandering underground stems in the same way as does *L. duchartrei*. Raising large numbers from seed and rigorous selection may be the way to find strains that are more amenable in cultivation.

Grand Paradise

Another example of a modern
hybrid lily that has great
vigour and a prolific flowering
habit, 'Grand Paradise' (left)
also exhibits a welcome
tolerance to wide ranges of soil
conditions. Dark stems and
rich clean polished foliage add
considerably to the image of a
big bold character. It looks
especially fine growing
amongst grey-leaved shrubs
such as *Senecio* 'Sunshine' and
lavenders.

Lilium longiflorum

This is the Easter lily,
traditionally used for church
decoration, and a florists'
favourite. In Britain it is
normally considered a
greenhouse plant, but it is
probably hardier than has been
thought – in warm regions in
parts of the United States,
Africa, and Australia it has
naturalized itself. Here (above
and right) it is growing in the
author's garden, in a cold spot
in the Midlands.

Lilium martagon cattaniae
This (above) is the most
distinctive variation in a
variable species – the depth
of pigment and unusual
lacquered finish of the flowers
differentiate it from its fellows
and from the type species. It is
as trustworthy a plant as any
from this foolproof species,
though bulbs that have been
out of the ground for a period
may sulk as a result and,
although they are busily
establishing roots below
ground, refuse to produce
stem or leaf above ground for
a season.

Lilium hansonii
Like *Lilium martagon*,
L. hansonii (above) is a lily of
great reliability. It is the
species thought by botanists to
be the closest to the original
founder protospecies of the lily
genus. It is a splendid plant,
relatively early into blossom.
Its thick petals do not recurve
as much as those of
L. martagon, with which it has
been crossed to produce
outstanding races of long-lived
garden lilies. Once settled it
will last decades without any
fussing.

Lilium wigginsii
Lilium wigginsii is a North American species, and a distinctive one that seems to adapt to cultivation better than many. Certainly it is able to produce tall stems with a great number of flowers, gracefully borne.

Lilium michauxii

Lilium michauxii is another American species. Although it is botanically close to *L. superbum*, it seems more tricky to cultivate than that species, although the attempt is well worth trying. It is probably best raised from seed.

Lilium szovitsianum

This is a first-rate garden plant, especially useful where it can be allowed to naturalize itself, which it does readily from its plentiful production of seeds. It is closely related to *Lilium monadelphum* and is now usually listed as a subspecies of that Caucasian lily. It is best introduced into the garden from freshly dug bulbs obtained from a nursery or neighbour, otherwise there will be a year's wait for it to produce stem growth.

Lilium leichtlinii maximowiczii

This is the better-known red-orange form of the yellow species used early on in the cross-breeding of Asiatic hybrids. It grows sturdily and is no sluggard in flowering.

Lilium lankongense
The grace and delicate colouring of *Lilium lankongense* (left), combined with a pleasing growth habit, make it a lovely plant to grow. The species is the cornerstone of the race of Asiatic hybrids bred by Dr North, with a pendent pose and scent that distinguish them from other Asiatic hybrids.

Lilium nepalense
This is one of the most theatrical lilies in a genus crowded with glamorous players. In temperate zones it is worth trying *Lilium nepalense* (right), although it may have to be grown under cool glass and tended with care. Seed is usually available and germinates readily – it is growing the resulting bulbs to flowering size that presents the challenge.

Lilium regale album
This variation (above) is supplied by nurserymen in the form of clones resulting from the selection from the species of individual plants that lack the usual wine colour in their buds. Some clones have been named. All are as easy and reliable in cultivation as is the species.

Tweedle-dee
'Tweedle-dee' (left) is a
strong, early-summer hybrid
that was bred in 1978 by the
Ministry of Agriculture
Horticultural Research Station
at Rosewarne, Cornwall. A
number of very fine hybrids
were bred at this station, many
of which were given Cornish
placenames, such as 'Redruth',
'Camborne', and 'Truro'.

La Bohème
Bred in 1965 from *Lilium lancifolium* and a hybrid derived from *L. bulbiferum croceum* × *L. hollandicum*, this useful and robust hybrid (left) is one of the many Asiatics that can be induced to give very large crops of bulbils in the leaf axils if flowers are sacrificed by early decapitation. It is interesting and reassuring to find old hybrids managing to compete sensibly with modern cultivars in the garden.

Lady Bowes Lyon
By common consent, this old hybrid (above) typifies the grace and bewitching beauty of Asiatics bred for garden use rather than for commercial purposes – the huge market for cut flowers demands tidy stems of upright blooms that look good in bud and pack well without fracturing. It may well be that it will be left to amateur raisers to develop the more graceful pendent lilies like 'Lady Bowes Lyon', while the professionals develop the stiffer commercials.

83

Troika
'Troika' is a very attractive
Asiatic hybrid with hanging
flowers. It is unusual in having
Lilium regale as a grandparent
– its breeding is 'Maxwell' ×
L. regale with 'Bronzino'.

Matchless

'Matchless', which was introduced in 1969, still maintains its fine reputation as a sturdy lily that blooms early and makes a good plant for both garden bed and container. Its compact strength is inherited through the parentage 'Enchantment' × 'Connecticut Lemonglow'.

Pirate

This excellent plant (left) has had a distinguished commercial career and is still grown in quantity for both the cut-flower and the garden trade. It is dark-leaved and dark-stemmed – colouring that makes it look splendidly healthy – and the stems are slender but very wiry. The neat flower form and bright colouring is much enhanced by the highly polished finish. It was bred in 1971 from the richly coloured 'Paprika' by pollen of a flower bred from 'Lemon Queen' × 'Mega'.

Discovery

'Discovery' (above) may have been the pollen parent of 'Pirate' – its own parents were certainly 'Lemon Queen' and 'Mega'. Its good-sized flowers and its charming pose make it a most lovely garden lily. It has a gentle, graceful image, partly because of its soft colouring, but it is a plant of abundant vigour.

Sterling Star

'Sterling Star' (left) has held its popularity ever since its introduction in 1972. Wiry stems and a pleasing open head of flowers commend it to flower arrangers, while its pointed, starry form, pale colouring, and beauty spots ensure the loyalty of the gardener.

Rosita

Lilium cernuum as its pollen parent has given 'Rosita' (right) delicate colouring and a somewhat more refined plant form than many popular Asiatics. Pink was a colouring missing from the range of earlier Asiatics, but 'Rosita' and an increasing number of other descendants of *L. cernuum* now offer various shades of pink to fill the gap.

North Hybrids

North hybrids (left) clearly show the influence of *Lilium lankongense* in that they are scented, a desirable quality that most Asiatics lack. They are all pendent and, although some, such as 'Rosemary North', are pastel-coloured, others, such as the mauve-pink 'Angela North', are more richly pigmented. Freedom of bloom and graceful habit make them enchanting garden plants in June and July.

Sunray

'Sunray' (above), introduced in 1965, is a Stone and Payne hybrid with the same parents, 'Connecticut Lass' and 'Keystone', as 'Connecticut King' and the same forthright constitution. Unlike its sibling, though, its flowers have a number of small dark freckles. Despite competition from many later introductions it is unlikely to be dislodged from its position as a favourite garden plant and cut flower.

Iona

'Iona' is a *Lilium lankongense*
hybrid with larger flowers than
many. Like most hybrids
descended from *L. lankongense*,
it bears its mid-summer
flowers a little later than most
Asiatics – and certainly later
than 'Enchantment'.

Peggy North
Another of the *Lilium lankongense* hybrids raised by Dr North and named after members of his family, 'Peggy North' is more strongly coloured than most. It shares a dislike of lime with other members of the family.

93

Theodore Haber
Bred in 1975 from the dark
Lilium martagon cattaniae by
the unusual species
L. tsingtauense, 'Theodore
Haber' (right) is a fascinating
cultivar whose richly coloured
flowers are so heavily
lacquered as to give them a
glassy look that can be
matched in the world of
flowers only perhaps by some
members of the orchid family.

Shuksan
After nearly three-quarters of
a century – it was named in
1933 – 'Shuksan' (far right) is
still revered as one of the most
outstanding hybrids of the
native American species. Its
parents are *Lilium humboldtii*
and *L. pardalinum*, and it has
inherited from them strength
and reliability.

94

African Queen
Originally, richly coloured selections of aurelian hybrids were marketed as a series or strain under the name African Queen. Later an outstanding individual plant was selected and propagated as a clone. It is this plant (left) that is now on sale as 'African Queen'.

Golden Clarion
These lilies, selections from the de Graaff hybridization programme, are richly coloured, wide-trumpeted varieties of great vigour – the stems photographed here (right) were from bulbs that had been growing contentedly in the same garden for thirty years, the only real attention given them being to split the clumps every few years.

Olympic Hybrids
Although originally the
Olympic strain comprised
trumpet flowers of various
colours, it has now become
standard practice to market
only the white hybrids (right)
under this name. They are of
mixed parentage and those
offered for sale may include
several clones.

Imperial Silver
The Imperial strains of
hybrids are three-quarters
Lilium auratum and one-
quarter *L. speciosum*, being
derived from the cross
L. speciosum × *L. auratum*
with *L. auratum*. The best of
the resulting seedlings were
segregated according to
colour. Imperial Silver (far
right) is snow-white, usually
with a generous number of
very tiny crimson-maroon
spots.

Imperial Gold
Imperial Gold (left) clones
have large white flowers
enlivened by a wide yellow
band, peppered with maroon
spots, down the centre of each
petal, more dominant in some
individual plants than in
others. Like all lilies of the
Imperial strain they are
heavily perfumed.

Imperial Crimson
Imperial Crimson (above),
too, is richly fragrant. Most
clones sold under this name
have flowers so heavily painted
with crimson that only a
narrow margin of white is left
on the petal, but the width of
the margin varies with the
individual.

Avignon

'Avignon' (left) is a strong Asiatic cultivar that is likely to need lifting every two or three seasons to divide up the clumps of bulbs so that they can be given more space and fresh soil.

Bald Eagle

'Bald Eagle' (right) is one of an ever-growing number of Oriental hybrids of very high quality – indeed the only major advance that seems worthwhile from the gardener's point of view is the breeding into them of a tolerance of lime.

Merci
The width of its flowers, its
good pose, and its delicate,
warm colouring make 'Merci'
(left) an especially attractive
lily and account for its
deserved popularity among
knowledgeable gardeners.

Black Beauty
Because it combines Oriental
blood with something quite
different – it comes from
Lilium speciosum × *L. henryi*
–'Black Beauty'' (right) is a
rarity among lily hybrids. It is
one of the darkest of all lilies
and for this reason is
sometimes better appreciated
growing in a container than in
the open.

Lilium davidii

Lilies of this Chinese species (right and far right) look rather like smaller, more refined tiger lilies. They played a very considerable part in the breeding of Asiatic hybrids, to which they donated a free-flowering habit and a pyramidical flower arrangement. They are, however, still worth growing for their own sakes. The foliage is dark and stems deep maroon, nearly black. Energetic bulbs can have many dozens of flowers – the author has counted over a hundred on outstanding stems. Virus-clean stock raised from seed soon reaches flowering size. It could still make sense to back-cross modern hybrids on to the species to get hybrids with many flowers in a well-spaced pyramid.

Journey's End

'Journey's End' was bred in 1957 from 'Phillipa' by *Lilium speciosum* 'Gilrey', so it has an impeccable *auratum-speciosum* pedigree. It is a superb lily, so good that arguably none of the modern hybrids has superseded it. It is strong in growth and healthy in appearance and its ease of culture is combined with a generous floral habit.

Medaillon
This is a popular hybrid of
unknown parentage but of
very well-known merit. It is an
upward-looking Asiatic that
flowers in early to mid-
summer and is of unobtrusive
medium height – 2ft 6in–3ft
(75–90cm). It is one of the
leading cut-flower varieties, as
well as being one of the leading
garden lilies – its quieter
colour is as easy to manage in
floral arrangements as it is in
garden colour combinations.

Prominence

'Prominence' is a sturdy, easy-to-grow variety, with narrow leaves, growing to about 2ft 6in (75cm). Because, like 'Medaillon', it has a more subtle colouring than many modern Asiatic hybrids it is, still, like 'Medaillon', a useful component in any garden colour scheme. Seen here growing in one of the author's beds of shallow soil over shaly rock; not ideal lily conditions!

Cherrywood

'Cherrywood', a hybrid of American species will occupy the ground for a very long time – increasing year after year and producing large numbers of flower spikes in each new season. It is a clone selected from among the Bullwood hybrids raised in England by Derek Fox from *Lilium pardalinum* with an American hybrid as pollen parent. It has spreading petals gently recurving to point upwards, but not inwards in the manner of *L. pardalinum* and most American hybrids.

6

PROPAGATION

Many bulbous plants increase remarkably easily, but having spent a lifetime working with bulbs I do not believe there is a plant so easy, so quick, and so diverse in its methods of increase as the lily. Its mission in life is to fill the world with beauty; it gets down to the job in real earnest. A pod of seeds may have well over a hundred fertile potential new plants. Ten or more scales can be removed from a good healthy bulb, each scale capable of producing one, two, or three quite sizable bulbils in a matter of weeks. Some lilies naturally produce large numbers of bulbils in the leaf axils, a hundred could be a modest number from a plant; others, although not normally bearing such bulbils, may be easily induced to do so. Some bulbs below ground increase steadily, others are quicker, still more are impatient. Stems that come straight up from the bulb may have that section below ground prolific with variously sized bulblets ready to start independent life after a season. In other types the stem wanders around and produces very sizable bulbs at intervals along its length before turning up into the daylight. Of course, lilies are perfect subjects for the laboratory techniques of meristem and tissue culture – techniques that, with care, can be transferred to the kitchen table. The lily's second name should be Fecundity.

Seeds

First among the advantages of growing new lilies from seed is that the young plants may be guaranteed free from disease. Virus is not passed on through seeds. Raising new stock from species will reproduce that kind within fairly restricted specific limits, but there is always the possibility of producing some improved variant by virtue of colour, form, or perhaps even more importantly, of hardiness and amenability. Hybrid seed will produce varying offspring, some good, some less good, some altogether more distinguished than the parents.

The disadvantages of seed raising are that it needs some care and that the seedlings will take some while to reach flowering maturity. The time taken from seed sowing to the first bloom depends partly on how well the seedlings are treated, and partly on the type – some lilies can be brought from seed to bloom within twelve months, some few others may take five to seven years.

There are four different ways in which lily seed germinates.

Above ground germination can take place within a few weeks, with a thin strip of leaf showing above the surface. This is the most popular with lilies, and gardeners! It is the epigeal-immediate method. Most Asiatics and Trumpets are of this class. The leaves use the food from the seeds, quickly lengthen, and appear above the ground as narrow green strap shapes. The seed case may still be held on the tip of each leaf. The first true, more rounded, leaf follows.

Below-ground germination means that the seed sends a tube down and forms a tiny bulb before turning up and producing a small leaf above the surface. If this is done at once it is the hypogeal immediate method.

Both above- and below-ground methods may be

subject to a period of delay of some months. Thus we have the epigeal-delayed, and the hypogeal-delayed methods. The hypogeal-delayed is the second largest class.

Seed of both the immediately germinating classes may be treated in the same way. Seed harvested up until mid-summer may be sown straightaway and will result in small bulbs by the end of the growing season. Seed saved in late August and after is best treated with fungicide and stored dry and cool until early February. Then it may be sown and the young plants grown on so that by the end of August there are healthy young bulbs that can be planted out and established before the worst of the winter arrives.

Treatment with a fungicide before sowing is a sensible precaution against initial troubles. An open gritty compost with plenty of peat will do nicely for the seed trays. Commercial mixes using sterilized soils are perfectly satisfactory. The seed should be covered only by the lightest dusting of compost. Something like a square inch, about six square centimetres, should be allowed for each seed so that it may grow quickly and have enough room to develop with several leaves before being moved. The germination rate for these immediate types is very high. Deep trays will be best, perhaps some 3in (8cm) deep will be fine. The greatest care needs to be taken to ensure no fungus troubles occur – good, airy conditions will help and any leaf showing signs of distress should immediately be removed and destroyed. Vigorous types will have formed bulbs 1–1½in (2.5–4cm) across by the end of August and these can be safely lined out in nursery lines in well-dug soil with plenty of humus in it.

Over-winter care is a matter of making sure the bulbs are kept moist, not sodden, and that they are protected from the worst of the frosts. It is possible to sow seeds of robust kinds like *L. regale* in frames or even outside. This species may show its first flower some eighteen months after sowing. The prudent will nip off this flower to prevent it seeding and to make sure that the plant gets on with the first priority, the building of larger bulbs that will produce stronger stems the following season.

Above-ground germinating lilies that are delayed include well-known species such as *L. candidum*, whose seed is best saved and sown in February, and others, such as *L. chalcedonicum*, *L. pomponium*, *L. pyrenaicum*, and *L. henryi*, whose seed can be sown immediately it is ripe, although it will take its time in germinating. Many of this class will appear at intervals. It could be that the first flush of seedlings will give you as many plants as you want and, if so, the rest may be jettisoned. Shyer and more precious seedlings can be pricked out as they become large enough to handle, leaving all as little disturbed as possible so that later-germinating ones can continue to develop.

The main lily that follows the below-ground delayed form of germination is *L. martagon* and its kin. Seeds of this type need twelve weeks of warmth at around 70°F (20°C) to initiate the formation of small bulbs. Then they need some six weeks of coolness, preferably just above freezing, to trigger off their leaf-producing metabolism. Seeds of *L. martagon* may be sown when ripe and then the last of the summer should provide the initial warm period. The following winter will give more than enough of the cool run. As this seed is slow to develop into reasonable-sized little bulbs, the whole sowing will need to stay in containers for two seasons.

Scales

This is probably the favourite method of increasing lilies for most gardeners. It is easy and does not need special equipment or skills. The advantages of reproducing by scales are that small bulblets will be formed in four to seven weeks and that these young bulbs can be intensively grown to provide flowering bulbs very quickly. Of course every plant produced will be a chip of the old block, with exactly the same genetic make up. Disadvantages are very few. The only real one is that if the parent bulb is diseased then you are propagating it and multiplying your troubles.

Trays two-thirds full of an equal mix of grit and peat can be used to receive the scales. These can be taken from a bulb to the extent of reducing it to half its weight. Any dried or diseased outer scales should be rejected and then the better ones snapped carefully away from the base, working in rotation around the bulb. Timing of the operation may vary. With the early-flowering kinds the most propitious period will be shortly after blooming, when the plant can be lifted and the scales removed before the depleted bulb is treated with fungicide and re-planted. Alternatively bulbs may be exposed in the ground and scales carefully taken without lifting the bulb, but this is obviously more awkward. It is perfectly possible to take scales of an Asiatic hybrid and to have some bulbs large enough to bloom the following year! Some kinds, such as the late flowering *L. speciosum*, are better dealt with in the spring so that the young bulblets can be growing on through the year; to wait until after flowering would mean starting in the late autumn, not the best time to get things moving fast.

All lilies may be increased by the scale method. Some may take longer to grow to flowering size, but this simply reflects their more measured attitude to growing generally. The Martagons are slower than most. It is interesting to note that the jointed scales of many American species and their hybrids will produce bulblets from complete scales or from the divided pieces fractured at their joints.

Scales are dusted or dampened with fungicide and pushed for two-thirds of their depth into the tray's compost. When the tray is full and labelled, a check is made that the compost is moist without being sodden, and then the whole enclosed in a clear polythene bag and kept in a temperature of between 60°F (15°C) and 70°F (20°C).

An alternative method is to mix the fungicide-treated scales with vermiculite in a polythene bag and to keep them warm, preferably at a steady 70°F (20°C). Odd scales at the edge of the mix will enable one to monitor progress. Surprisingly soon, bulblets will start to form along the callused bottom of each scale. After some weeks, many may start making roots and beginning to extrude small leaves. At this stage they need taking out and growing on either outside in a nursery row, in frames, or in containers with a humus-rich growing compost.

Bulbils

Some few species and hybrids carry lots of bulbils in their leaf axils. Notable for this are *L. lancifolium*, *L. bulbiferum*, *L. sulphureum*, and *L. sargentiae*. Many others can be induced to adopt this easy and prolific way of increasing by variations of basically

the same method. If the flowering top of the stem is cut away as soon as the buds are visible, the energies of the plant seem to be displaced in favour of producing bulbils. This happens with many of the Asiatic hybrids, not only those with the blood of *L. lancifolium* in them. Virtually all the Asiatic hybrids at present available can be induced to produce bulbils. Somewhat more surprisingly it will also work with species like *L. auratum*, *L. candidum*, *L. centifolium*, *L. chalcedonicum*, *L. dauricum*, and *L. leichtlinii* together with their hybrids such as *L. × testaceum*, and the early hybrid series *L. × maculatum* and *L. × hollandicum*. Aurelian hybrids bred from the crossing of *L. henryi* with Trumpet species are prolific.

If the raising of many plants is the aim, it is worth mentioning that a greater proportion of bulbils can be harvested from smaller bulbs. Naturally a greater number of these small bulbs can be accommodated in a particular area. The procedure recommended is to take the healthy bulb to be propagated, and to reproduce it first by scaling. The resulting small bulbils are then grown strongly to give a series of vigorous but still undersized bulbs that can then be grown on for stem bulbils.

By using this artificial method of producing stem bulbils under glass it is possible to have them ready to grow on much earlier than in the open. This obviates the main problem with many of those harvested from the open, that they only ripen late in the season when it is difficult or impossible to get the young plants established before winter. There is also another possible benefit. Closer examination and control under glass will make it easier to watch for disease and to take steps if trouble threatens.

Bulbils are harvested when ripe, that is when they may be easily detached from the leaf axil just before they start dropping. They may be grown on in normal lily composts in containers under cool glass, lined out in frames, or even in the open. They will rapidly produce roots and leaves, the bulbs swelling very satisfactorily. As with all methods of reproduction the idea is to get the plants into rapid action and established before the winter. In the open the young plants may need protection from the effects of frosts. Usually they will stand all the cold but they will be pulled up by the expansion and thawing of the top soil due to frost so that they are left stranded and very vulnerable. Straw, bracken waste, frame lights, or anything to keep them slightly drier than the surrounding sodden soil and to keep out the worst of the frost will help significantly.

Of the stronger growing types it is possible to have flowering bulbs after one full growing season.

Stem Bulbs

Underground bulbs are formed on the stems of a considerable number of lily species and hybrids. The size of these on any one stem may vary from some well on their way to flowering-sized plants to tiny ones that will need careful handling even if they are worth using at all. Many of the commercially propagated species and hybrids will have their stem bulbs removed when lifted, graded by size, and grown on for one or two seasons to provide future saleable stock. Species that are notable for their underground stem bulbs include *L. auratum, L. brownii, L. dauricum, L. davidii, L. henryi, L. lancifolium, L. longiflorum,* and *L. speciosum.* Hybrids of any of these species are likely to be good stem-bulb producers and so the energetic Asiatic hybrids will be well to the fore. The more vigorously the plants are grown the more bulbs are likely to be produced, but their number will be significantly increased if the parent bulbs are planted deeply so that there is a much longer length of underground stem growing through gritty humus-rich compost.

Exploitation of this source of bulbs is possible by lifting bulbs immediately after flowering and severing the stems from the bulbs either by pulling them out of the bulbs or by cutting them as low as possible. Bulbs are replanted. The severed stems are then carefully replanted at least as deeply as before, well watered, and kept growing as strongly as possible. This applies to all those that produce strong stem-rooting systems and have begun to produce bulblets at the time of post-flowering lifting. Now all the leaves and roots will be working to store food in the bulblets and not dividing the result of their labours between these and the mother bulb. By the end of the summer there may well be a very pleasing harvest of bulbs possibly nearly a year more mature than those of the unsevered stems.

Division

Gardeners who have not yet succumbed to the fascination of lily culture might think that division would be the first and most obvious method of propagation. They will see their clumps of lilies becoming thicker and in need of more room. They will work on the age-old principle of divide and rule. Rule, in the gardening sense, is a matter of keeping control of the plants and allocating each the maximum scope for display allowable in the competitive arena of the garden's confines. Division is best done a few weeks after flowering. The clump is gently eased up by forking all the way round, the idea being to raise the mass of bulbs with as much lively root as possible. Topsoil is worked away from the lifted clump to reveal the number of bulbs below. These may be teased apart carefully and re-planted immediately. There may be some bulbs still joined Siamese-twin-wise but clearly in need of a simple operation to start independent careers. A sharp knife through the joining tissue will do the trick, the exposed tissue being dusted or dampened with fungicide. It is sensible to remove the old flowering top. This makes the whole new plant less liable to being rocked in the wind and looks tidier.

American species, such as *L. pardalinum,* that form rhizomatous mats of tough scale-lined tissue, may be propagated some weeks after flowering or in the late winter before getting into rapid active growth. Scales are very brittle and, as valuable foodstores, need to be husbanded. Care therefore is needed in lifting or exposing part of the rhizomatous growth. Having got it in an operable state, each growing point of the branching rhizome may be taken to be a potential new plant. The rhizome may be cut and the new plant removed carefully to be replanted. As much of the old rhizome as possible should be taken with the new growing point, the point of severance being close to the rootstock from which it has branched. It may well be thought best to take a section of the complex so that the new plantation starts with more than one growing point.

Normal aftercare procedures should be adopted. The new plants should be watered thoroughly. They should be given reasonable soil and mulches. Weeds should be kept down.

Tissue Culture

Tissue-culture techniques are being used increasingly by keen amateur growers for two purposes. The first is to increase dramatically stock of special kinds. The second is to raise fresh individuals from the embryos within unripe seeds, a process that speeds up the production of the new plant and overcomes difficulties that cause some seed to die in the pod. If you raise an outstandingly important seedling you may wish to propagate it quickly yourself, though you can choose to hand it over to a professional firm that will undertake to produce whatever number you require. Obviously it will be cheaper to do the job yourself and will give greater satisfaction. Professionals are sometimes called upon to revitalize a virused stock. Under an electron microscope the meristem of a bulb is cut out to give virus-free tissue which can be cloned to provide the basis for a clean stock.

The overriding concern with all tissue culture is to ensure that at no time can cultures be contaminated by the ever-present organisms, mainly bacterial or fungal, that will kill. Hygiene is necessary at all times.

Embryo Culture

The aim is to remove the embryos from the unripe seed in pods approximately fifty days after pollination, and to transfer them to a culture medium in sealed tubes to grow into small plants before being introduced to normal seedling-growing conditions.

Seed pods are collected green before any splitting. The pod is cut open and the rod-shaped potential plants in the centre of the seeds cut out using a small sharp scalpel or hobby knife. This operation is done under the sterile conditions of a cabinet as explained later, taking care to wash tools, hands, and arms with alcohol to sterilize them before any work is undertaken. Each embryo is introduced into its tube of sterile culture and will grow to a seedling-sized plant by the time the seed would have taken to ripen on the plant. The technique is especially useful for crosses, such as those using *L. lankongense*, where fertilization may have taken place but the seed cells outside the embryo collapse before ripening and the seeds become worthless husks. It is useful also with hypogeally germinating seed that normally needs periods of warmth and cold before germinating and beginning to form small bulbs. Months can be saved.

Some crosses between disparate lilies may produce small amounts of unusual-looking seed which is likely to come to nothing treated conventionally. Embryos may be rescued and potentially important hybrids grown on.

Equipment and Working Conditions

The need for sterile working conditions is the major factor in the success of tissue culture. Professionals will have laminarflow cabinets and powerful microscopes. Amateurs can improvise a cabinet or case that can be made sterile. The cabinet needs to have two holes through which the hands can enter to manipulate the contents and the holes must be protected by rubber or plastic flaps to prevent the introduction of infected air. It needs a window to view through. Inside there needs to be an ultraviolet germicidal light to surface-sterilize everything inside. In addition a small fluorescent light makes for even illumination. A working shelf of frosted glass with a light source below will be necessary to view clearly the seed and tissue being cut and manipulated. To work with comfort the cabinet will need to be about 2ft (60cm) long to allow space for the hand holes. Depth and height will range from 1ft (30cm) to 1ft 6in (45cm). Our own cabinet we lined inside with kitchen foil to provide a surface easy to keep sterile.

Other necessities will be a scalpel or hobby knife, a quantity of culture tubes, a litre measuring glass, a saucepan with lid, a domestic pressure cooker, indelible marker pen, culture mediums, and a quantity of alcohol to wash hands, arms, tools, etc. An extra safeguard is a flame burner through which the cutting blade can be passed before cutting any tissue. A magnifying glass may well be a useful aid when freeing embryos from green seed.

The basis for culture media is agar derived from seaweed. To this should be added sucrose and water. The quantities are:

2 pints (1 litre)	distilled water
3½ teaspoons (6–8 grams)	agar
5 teaspoons (30 grams)	sugar

To this will be added dehydrated basic Murashige & Skoog 1862 culture for use with embryos. For propagation culture add the Enriched Lily Multiplication Media formulated by Dr Toshia Murashige. (These cultures are available from various commercial sources, such as Microplants Ltd, Longnor, Buxton, Derbyshire.)

The ingredients are placed in a saucepan and brought to a gentle boil. They are allowed to simmer until all is dissolved. Stirring will hasten the process, which will be complete when the mix becomes clear. For the best results we need a pH level of 5.5–6. Using indicator papers we can test it. If too acid, add drops of dilute potassium hydroxide until corrected. If too alkaline, drops of dilute hydrochloric acid are added.

Culture tubes may be glass or plastic but should be capable of being treated in a pressure cooker. Normally 16mm tubes will be a handy size. If test tubes are used they can be plugged with cotton wool or capped with foil. Tubes should be one-third filled with the culture medium, about 2 teaspoonfuls (10ml), and capped or plugged. 1 litre of culture medium should be enough for 100 tubes. Now the tubes are sterilized by packing them upright in tin cans and placing them in a pressure cooker with 4–6 pints of water and 'cooking' them for twenty minutes at 15 pounds pressure. The cooker is allowed to cool before opening.

Multiplication Culture
Under ideal conditions a few pieces of bulb scale may give rise to thousands of small bulbs within a few months. While bulb scales are the most obvious source of tissue, young leaves, ovaries, or even fresh flower petals can be cultured to give new bulbs.

It is easiest to remove the outer scales of the bulb to be processed and to use only the inner, cleaner, fresher ones. Each of these to be used is thoroughly washed in distilled or boiled water. They are then surface-sterilized by being immersed in a solution of fungicide, such as Benlate or Janola, for thirty minutes. Ten minutes in a 10 per cent solution of laundry bleach will do the same job. You may choose, either to cut the scales into small chunks to produce bulbils which are then recut into many smaller pieces to introduce into culture, or you can

cut the original scale into these small pieces in the first place. Choosing the first method entails cutting the scales into pieces less than $\frac{1}{2}$in (10mm) square, under sterile conditions. These pieces are placed in Petri dishes, jars, or tubes of culture medium and kept at a temperature of 70°F (21°C). This will give lots of small bulblets after six weeks. It is important to label all cultures indelibly to avoid any confusion.

Under sterile conditions the bulblets are cut free from the parent tissue and divided into pieces only $\frac{1}{8}$in (2mm) square but not smaller. Each piece is introduced into a culture tube and allowed to produce plants at the same temperature as before. In this way it is possible to arrange five generations of lilies within a year, a process that would take something like fifteen years by natural means.

Young plants are grown in the tubes until they have leaves and a developed root system. This will take between eight and fourteen weeks. At this stage they are taken from the tubes, washed thoroughly with clean water, soaked in a fungicide such as Captan, and then planted up in a mix of equal parts of coarse peat, sterilized soil, and rough sand or grit. They are grown on in a greenhouse or under similar shelter until they are larger and hardy enough to plant outside. Under ideal conditions it has proved possible to have plants blooming before twelve months have passed from the date of culturing.

The stages are:

1 Prepare culture tubes by filling one-third with medium and sealing.
2 Turn on ultraviolet light in cabinet two hours before work.
3 Remove undamaged scales from bulb.
4 Wash and surface-sterilize scales.
5 Cut scales into small pieces and introduce into culture medium.
6 Keep culture tubes at 70°F (21°C) until plants have grown leaves and roots.
7 Wash plants free of culture, dip in fungicide, plant in growing medium.

Hybridization
Most lilies hybridize readily and the results can be most exciting. Hybrids from species may well be more amenable garden plants and, for instance, may

have a far greater tolerance of pH levels than the parents. Flower forms, poses, colours, and sizes can be varied. Improvements may be made in plant habit, the stems can be strengthened and the foliage made more attractive. Plants may be more prolific of blooms, having more per stem, and, because bulbs increase quicker, more stems.

Amateur breeders have the opportunity to look at the family as a whole and to decide specific areas that they feel may be worth exploring and exploiting. It could be that the idea of a range of small early-flowering plants appeals, the sort of thing that would look well in the garden but that may be overlooked by the commercial breeder. Lovely garden kinds bred from *L. martagon* and *L. hansonii* are still far from having had their potential fully exploited. Similarly, the long-lived American species can produce wonderful flowers for mid-summer display, stylized and breathtaking in their beauty.

Techniques are simple. Pollen is transferred from the anthers of one parent to the stigmas of the other just by holding an anther in tweezers and dabbing the receptive sticky stigma with the pollen. As lily pods are capable of producing large amounts of seed, there may well be no need to pollinate many flowers when making a particular cross. If the seed parent is going to bloom much later than the pollen parent, anthers may be stored if taken when ripe, placed dry in a plastic or glass phial, and kept in the domestic refrigerator. Pollen may be stored for several weeks or months.

Fungus invading seed pods may be a problem. Early fungicide sprays should preclude any infection. Once a pod has become infected the seeds are rendered useless by the fungus mycelium's penetration.

The chances of raising good new plants from hybridizing are very good indeed. Have you ever seen an ugly lily? By bringing into play the less-used species you may well be tapping new genetic potential that will give something distinctive. In the past many world-famous lilies have been bred in small amateur gardens and there seems no reason why this should not continue.

One of the major obstacles to lily cultivation for some gardeners is the presence of lime in their soil. The breeding of lilies that do not object to lime can be undertaken in several ways. Modern Asiatic hybrids seem to be more tolerant of lime than their ancestors. New cultivars bred from the Russian hybrid 'Fialkovaya' will have the blood of the lime-loving *L. monadelphum szovitsianum* in their breeding to give them a head start. Reproducing the *L. × testaceum* hybrid from *L. candidum* and *L. chalcedonicum* and the interbreeding of their offspring produces lovely kinds that enjoy limey soils. With Asiatic blood having been recently linked with that of *L. candidum* all sorts of exciting things might emerge from this complex.

The Orientals have long been cherished as the most exotic of all lilies, but they have been the most sensitive to lime. Very lime-tolerant *L. henryi* has been introduced into their breeding via the cultivar 'Black Beauty'. After many attempts, a tetraploid form of this hybrid has been mated with an Oriental to produce 'Beauty's Baby', a kind that seems to be very much more fertile and has given seed by a number of Orientals. The seedlings appear to be inheriting tolerance to lime.

One of the problems that amateur breeders need to be aware of is that a number of species will form seed without having their egg cells fertilized by pollen. Chief offenders are *L. canadense*, *L. davidii willmottiae*, *L. longiflorum*, *L. pumilum*, *L. regale*, *L. superbum*, *L. speciosum* and *L. szovitsianum*. If tempted to make use of these it may be sensible to try them as pollen parents. However, many of the problems associated with these have been overcome by luck or judgement and hybrids are usually available that can be used to introduce the genetic potential of the species. Thus the early flowering *L. pumilum* has been brought into play by Judith McRae and others, and these hybrids are fertile.

Sometimes the problem of apparent incompatibility is due to the fact that pollen grains have not enough energy to grow down long styles to the ovaries. Lilies with short styles may produce pollen able to travel this distance but no further. The answer may be to reduce the length of the style of the fancied seed parent by slicing a length off and applying the pollen to the cut surface.

Another problem is the collapse of seed within the pod of a cross-pollinated flower. Embryos may have been properly formed but the other cells of the seed fail. Embryo culture will enable unions to succeed that would otherwise be impossible.

Certain species and their offspring may have very important characteristics to introduce into breeding lines. For example *L. henryi* is likely to give a good resistance to virus diseases while also donating a tolerance to lime in soil. *L. candidum* may help to give hybrids with exceptional tolerance to low temperatures and low light intensities.

Benefits and drawbacks of some species are briefly summarized here. These factors may play some part in their hybrids, but on the whole the farther away from the species we move the less the inhibitions or advantages are felt.

L. amabile One of the most potent species in the early breeding of Asiatics. It proved readily compatible to the Asiatic species including *L. concolor*. It gives good disease resistance, with flowers that are brightly coloured and have the benefit of a lacquered finish. In several ways a more beneficial influence than *L. davidii*.

L. bulbiferum It has crossed easily with *L. wilsonii* and *L. dauricum*, and less readily with *L. davidii*, *L. lancifolium* and *L. leichtlii maximowiczii*. It is tolerant of lime, and helps to give strong, sturdy hybrids.

L. callosum This is the smallest-flowered Asiatic and when using its pollen it will be necessary to cut down the style of the seed parent. It will cross with *L. amabile*, *L. concolor*, *L. dauricum* and *L. pumilum*. It is late blooming and so may need to be grown under glass to be brought into bloom early enough to use. It may be easier to use its genetic potential via existing hybrids with *L. concolor* and *L. pumilum*.

L. cernuum The drawbacks to using *L. cernuum* are that it is very susceptible to virus and has very narrow foliage. It has been useful in introducing white and pastel shades to the Asiatics. Its water-soluble pigment, anthocyacin, if combined with the carotine pigments of yellow and orange lilies gives first-generation seedlings likely to be dull coloured. It crosses with *L. davidii* and related species, and with *L. dauricum* if embryo culture is used.

L. concolor This small lily is difficult to interbreed with other species, though it is compatible under very good conditions with *L. pumilum* and *L. callosum*. Its influence is probably best exploited through existing hybrids.

L. davidii This will cross with all Asian species except *L. concolor*. A strong point is its tolerance to virus. It is very dominant in breeding, in transmitting colour, pose, spotting, and narrow foliage. Better results are probable using *L. davidii* seedlings.

L. dauricum Extreme hardiness and earliness are passed to hybrids. The species is very variable. It will mate easily with all Asians except *L. concolor*. The combination of this species with *L. leichtlinii maximowiczii* has proved a good cornerstone in breeding.

L. lancifolium Will give seed by pollen of *L. amabile*, *L. bulbiferum*, *L. davidii* and their hybrids. Dark foliage and stems are likely to be passed on, together with a tolerance to virus. Triploid forms are probably all hybrids with *L. leichtlinii maximowiczii*.

L. lankongense Has produced hybrids with *L. cernuum*, *L. davidii*, *L. duchartrei* and *L. leichtlinii maximowiczii*. Embryo culture is usually needed. Hybrids are likely to be sterile but may respond to embryo culture.

L. leichtlinii and **L. l. maximowiczii** These are fertile with most Asians and give robust, wide-petalled hybrids with good virus tolerance.

L. pumilum This is compatible, using pollen, to *L. amabile*, *L. bulbiferum*, *L. concolor*, *L. dauricum*, *L. davidii* and to *L. cernuum* by embryo culture.

L. wardii Very difficult to use. It has crossed with 'Oddball'.

L. wilsonii (and **L. w. flavum**) An important species in early Asiatic breeding. Both forms are late flowering and so are best grown under glass if they are to be used in breeding. Vigorous plants have been raised by back-crossing some of the Connecticut series to either of the wild plants.

Perhaps the greatest problem for amateur breeders is that all their seedlings are swans, with not a single ugly duckling among them. The picking of a winner or winners is hard. It could be a help to consult other lily fanciers. You can ask their advice; like all advice you may, or may not, decide to accept it.

SPECIES LILIES

Classification

The word 'lily' has been used very vaguely, often for bulbous flowers that do not even belong to the Liliaceae family. In this book, though we use it only for members of the *Lilium* genus and have not even stretched a point to include the giant Himalayan 'lily', *Cardiocrinum giganteum*.

Early attempts at lily classification following the Linnaean system depended heavily on the form of the flowers and their pose. It was always a heavily compromised system, with little inherent botanical rationality, but with the flood of new types arriving from east and west during the late 19th and the 20th centuries all pretensions to any kind of sense broke down.

Lily growers owe an immense debt of gratitude to H. F. Comber, who published a completely revised system of classification in the 1949 *Lily Yearbook* of the Royal Horticultural Society. Herbarium specimens were certainly examined but the work relied on a careful examination of all the kinds then available as living specimens. Comber first listed the features upon which his classification was based, and then divided the genus into seven main groups, the larger of these groups being subdivided.

No groups of living organisms at different stages of evolutionary differentiation are ever going to fall exactly into tidy compartments without some questions being left partially unanswered, but this arrangement of Comber's comes as near to precision as one could possibly hope. It certainly matches what is thought to have been the evolutionary development of the genus. Comber's work has almost made nature seem tidy minded. This is, in fact, an over-simplification, as a consideration of some of the rare species growing on the uplands of the borders of Burma, India, and Tibet clearly demonstrates. Plants such as *L. mackliniae*, *L. amoenum*, *L. sherriffiae*, *L. sempervivoideum* and *L. henricii* confound the taxonomist by dawdling about on the borders of the *Fritillaria* and *Nomocharis* genera. *L. sherriffiae* has nodding blossoms that dare to share the chequered-print pattern of the dress of some fritillaries. Evolution has not yet provided a great divide between the genera.

Fifteen characteristics are seen to be essential in determining the classification. 1 germination, below or above ground. 2 germination, immediate or delayed. 3 leaves, in whorls or scattered on the stem 4 bulb scales, jointed or entire. 5 seeds, heavy or light. 6 bulb shape, erect and round, sub-rhizomatous, rhizomatous, or stoloniferous. 7 petals, with or without raised points, papillae. 8 nectary, with or without soft hairs. 9 flower form, turk's-cap or trumpet. 10 bulb colour, white or purple. 11 stem erect or creeping below ground. 12 leaf stalks obvious or not. 13 stigma, large or small. 14 stems, do or do not form roots. 15 one or sometimes two stems per bulb.

Characteristics are listed more or less in their order of importance, although certain of them may take on a greater significance in relation to some species or groups. It will be seen that the flower form appears only as ninth in the list and that flower pose does not enter into consideration at all.

Using these criteria, the seventy to eighty good species fall into seven groups.

Distribution

Lilies are wild plants of the northern hemisphere whose original centre of distribution would seem to have been somewhere in mainland Asia. *L. pumilum* and *L. callosum* range the farthest north – to 68° – in Manchuria and Siberia. *L. hansonii*, thought to be the nearest to the ancient prototype species of the genus, is found on the island of Ullŭng-do off the east coast of Korea. Korea is the home of several species including *L. amabile*, *L. callosum*, *L. cernuum*, *L. concolor*, *L. dauricum*, *L. distichum* and *L. tsingtauense*. Several species grow wild through the islands of Japan, including the horticulturally important *L. auratum* and *L. speciosum*, and also *L. japonicum*, *L. dauricum*, *L. leichtlinii*, *L. maximowiczii*, *L. medeoloides*, *L. rubellum*, and the well-known florist's white Trumpet, *L. longiflorum*, together with the rarer Trumpet, *L. nobilissimum*. Other Trumpets, including *L. formosanum*, and *L. philippinense* are found on the Pacific islands.

China's huge landmass is home to many lilies. Inland and to the north there are *L. brownii*, *L. davidii*, *L. duchartrei*, and *L. pumilum*. To the northeast are *L. brownii*, *L. concolor*, *L. lancifolium*, *L. medeoloides*, *L. pumilum*, and *L. tsingtauense*. The broad central mass is the home of *L. bakeriana*, *L. brownii*, *L. callosum*, *L. concolor*, *L. henryi*, *L. leucanthum*, *L. primulinum* and *L. speciosum*. The highlands of western China into Tibet and to the borders of Vietnam, Laos, Cambodia, and Burma are the homes of some of the small nomocharis-like species, such as *L. amoenum*, *L. henricii*, and *L. sempervivoideum*, as well as *L. brownii*, *L. davidii*, *L. duchartrei*, *L. lankongense*, *L. papilliferum*, *L. primulinum*, *L. regale*, *L. sargentiae*, *L. taliense* and *L. wardii*. Yunnan has over a dozen species. From northern Burma come the Trumpet *L. sulphureum* and the dainty *L. mackliniae*. From the Himalayas come the species *L. nepalense*, *L. polyphyllum*, and *L. wallichianum*. *L. neilgherrense* grows in southern India, just a mere 10° above the equator.

Globetrotter extraordinary *L. martagon* is the most nomadic of all. North of the Gobi desert from Siberia down to the Caucasus mountains and into Europe it treks through Latvia into Poland, Germany, France, the Iberian peninsula, and reaches into Hungary, Czechoslavakia, northern Italy, and Switzerland. This is unchallengeably the widest distribution of any single species.

Among the fascinating flora of the Caucasus and western Asia are found the species *L. candidum*, *L. ledebourii*, *L. martagon*, *L. monadelphum*, *L. polyphyllum*, and *L. ponticum*. In places *L. monadelphum* and its close relative *L. szovitsianum* can paint hillsides yellow. European species include *L. bulbiferum*, *L. candidum*, *L. carniolicum*, *L. chalcedonicum*, *L. martagon*, *L. pomponium* and *L. pyrenaicum*.

This leaves one isolated group, the American species, whose habitats vary from close by the seashore to high up mountainsides. If they have anything in common it

would be that nowhere are the bulbs left to struggle in boggy conditions. They may have plenty of moisture around their roots when growing, possibly from melting snows higher up, but they are kept relatively dry in the winter. While occasionally growing in light woodland, they are usually in places where they enjoy plenty of air and light and where, although their roots may be shaded by scrub, they enjoy good air, drainage and sunshine.

We look at each of the main groups in turn.

Martagon Group

Species of this group belong mainly to Japan and Korea. Group membership is shown by the whorled foliage and upright stems carrying smallish smooth-petalled flowers. Flowers are pendent, except in *L. tsingtauense*. The group is dominated by *L. martagon* (see page 38) which has more than once been claimed as native to Britain, although most would think this an unjustified assessment. True, it is found wild in a few spots in Britain, but only as a naturalized plant or garden escape.

Most gardeners would think themselves much the poorer for not having some Martagons growing somewhere in their territory. They are undemanding plants as far as soil is concerned, they will grow in a wide range of pH values, and do not worry about lime. New bulbs that have been held in store may take a while to settle. Sometimes the bulbs spend the first year making roots, without making any top growth. Thereafter they grow and increase steadily, but they are best left well alone to get on with the job. If they have to be moved, this can be done soon after blooming without losing a year's bloom.

First flower stems may carry just a few flowers, but stems from strong, established bulbs may have over fifty curled-up blossoms in the long candelabra arrangement. There are variations in the heights of the plants and the flower colours, but the surprise is that there is not more variation with such a widespread species. Stems may be 3–6ft (1–2m) high, the more-or-less standard mauve colour can be replaced by various shades, including ivory whites and very dark maroons. These dark-flowered lilies are given varietal status as *L. m. cattaniae* (see page 74). Usually the very dark maroon is combined with a high-gloss finish to make the flowers especially effective. New plants from seed or scales take four to seven years to reach flowering size.

Nearest to *L. martagon* is the tough *L. hansonii* (see page 74), one of the easiest of lilies to grow. In stance it is much like the martagon, with plenty of dark leaves in well-displayed whorls, but the flowers are a rusty golden tangerine and the petals, although reflexing, do not roll up into balls. Thick texture is as obvious as the generous freckling. The fact that the petals do not curl back too far makes more of the inflorescence. A dozen or more flowers are displayed in a narrow pyramid at a height of around 4–5ft (1.2–1.5m). It is indifferent to lime in the soil and is a regular mating partner of *L. martagon*.

L. hansonii is a species for everyone. Sturdy, very long lived, and a regular increaser, it has plenty of yeoman virtues. Because it is a very strong stem rooter and is inclined to produce a good quota of bulblets on this underground stem, it is politic to plant bulbs deeply. By careful excavation you may take your harvest of bulblets without lifting the bulbs. A strong group or two of this species looks well in the early summer.

Both *L. distichum* and *L. medeoloides* are much slighter plants than the foregoing species. They are both normally quite happy to sport only a single whorl of leaves but may augment this by having a few scattered ones above. *L. distichum* is usually the taller, but still no giant, varying between 20in (50cm) and an exceptional 3ft (1m). The lower stem is usually somewhat roughened, a point of distinction from *L. medeoloides*. In midsummer a few flowers are opened in a horizontal or somewhat depressed angle. Tangerine or pale red petals spread widely and then recurve. They can be lightly spotted. The stem-rooting bulbs enjoy a leafy soil, with good drainage in a cool spot. *L. medeoloides* is of the same obvious Martagon form, but it is a dwarf version, reaching only 1–2ft (30–60cm); it has a single whorl of leaves like a swirled skirt and three to six blooms, occasionally more. Orange or reddish pendent flowers have recurving petals, but they are not curled up. They are likely to have a sprinkling only of dark spots.

American Group

Early migration of ancestor types from Asia to America via the then-joined landmasses resulted in about two dozen species evolving in the New World. Most of them have whorled leaves, upright stems, and flowers with smooth petals. Many are to be found in the mountains that parallel the Pacific coastline. The series of valleys and high ridges isolated different lilies so that they became differentiated in their geographical vastnesses with no fraternization possible until they reached the ends of the mountain ranges.

Lilies are found in many parts of America, meeting various climatic conditions. Often the bulbs grow deeply in the ground and so are able in spring and early summer to tap moving underground water derived from melting snows and early rainfalls. This may be in a time of active growth and flowering, when they could go months without rain. The depth of the bulbs protects them from harsh winter cold, with the thermometer plunging many degrees below freezing point. They probably have a thick insulating blanket of snow for weeks during these worst of times.

These Americans are an interesting lot, but because of their preference for the conditions of their native stations they are not always the easiest of kinds to grow in some gardens. On the other hand some are among the easiest of all the genus.

Foremost as a garden plant because of its ease of culture, its very quick rate of increase, and its obvious good looks, is the leopard lily, *L. pardalinum* (see page 48), which comes from the coastal mountain ranges of California. It is a variable plant save in its universal good nature and attractiveness. Stems grow strongly erect, with polished grass-green leaves in tidy whorls. Buds are pendent and flowers either slightly pendent or facing outward to display their wide-opened, heavily spotted faces. Petals recurve so that tips may touch. In typical forms the colour is a rich tangerine-gold in the centre half and scarlet in the other half. These blooms are large, each petal being perhaps as much as 3½in (10cm) long, and made more conspicuous by the prominent protruded stamens, which are purple-red when new but are soon bright orange with pollen. Each 4–7ft (1.2–2.1m) stem carries several flowers, and as the plant is very vigorous and soon produces plenty of stems, the effect in July is very impressive.

This is the prime example of a rhizomatous lily. A piece with one bud will manage in a single season to grow forward to make two, three, four, or five new buds, and at this energetic rate of production can become crowded in three years and need splitting up again. *L. pardalinum* clones enjoy plenty of moisture when growing and appear happy in a wide variety of soils, but they are best suited by well-drained, moist soil with plenty of leaf mould or humus. Plants do not like a windy spot but are resentful of considerable shade. Bulbs should be planted with at least 4–5in (10–12cm) over their tops.

In catalogues and lists the next lily will be *L. pardalinum giganteum*. This has long been grown in gardens as an outstandingly robust and attractive plant. It has stems like vigorous bamboos going up to 7–8ft (2–2.5m). The plant is a hybrid known since 1890 and probably the result of an alliance with *L. humboldtii*. Stems carry six to a dozen flowers normally, but there are records of thirty to a stem. They are of the same general form as *L. pardalinum* but perhaps a little more pendent, the golden centre contrasting with heavy, dark purple spotting and crimson tips. The rhizomatous mats of bulbs grow with most satisfying speed.

Coming farther away from the coast but parallel with

it is the mountain range of the Sierra Nevada, which gives it name to the next related species, *L. nevadense*. Also close to *L. pardalinum* are the species *L. columbianum* and *L. humboldtii* with *L. ocellatum*, which most will regard as a good species in its own right but has often been listed as *L. humboldtii ocellatum*. All these species look close to *L. pardalinum*; they have clean upright stems with clearly whorled foliage and curving pendent flowers.

There is a group of plants related to *L. nevadense* but more distinct in their floral manners; these are *L. kelloggii*, *L. washingtonianum*, *L. rubescens*, and *L. bolanderii*. Even more individualistic are the botanical curiosities *L. philadelphicum* and *L. catesbaei*. *L. occidentale* has much of the *L. pardalinum* look but shows some affinity to *L. superbum* and *L. canadense*.

L. nevadense is an altogether slighter plant than *L. pardalinum*, with stems usually content with a 2–3ft (30–60cm) extension but capable of doubling this. The smaller, recurved flowers are of tangerine-gold tipped with red. *L. kelloggii* is in the same height range and usually has from one or two to over a dozen martagon-type flowers. In bud they are ivory-white, but they become flushed with mauve-pink after opening and age to a deepish purple; they are dotted with lots of little deep maroon spots. This same pigmentation is seen in the species *L. washingtonianum* and *L. rubescens*. In the first of these the flowers are carried on stems perhaps 4ft (1.2m) high, the petals forming funnel shapes before opening out. Any number up to twenty of these may be held horizontally in early and mid-summer. Starting pure white with a peppering of purple in the throats, they become more and more lilac-purple as they age.

L. washingtonianum purpurascens is generally thought to be an easier plant. It has more leaves than the type and the flowers, although perhaps a little shorter, have overlapping petals. They open white or shaded purple, but soon become a more bibulous wine colour. *L. rubescens* is held to be an easier plant still. It is variable in height and in the number of flowers held; a stem of 3–5ft (1–1.5m) would be average, with a dozen widely opening flowers that look upward. They open white or blush-mauve dotted with purple and become darker with age. Like *L. nevadense*, *L. kelloggii* and *L. washingtonianum* they are scented, an attribute that *L. pardalinum* lacks.

Quite a number of these species are rare or are not at present in wide cultivation, but their seed is sometimes offered by enterprising seedsmen and it is always worth experimenting to try to raise bulbs that may settle in the garden much better than written lore suggests.

It would be wonderful to get the rare *L. bolanderii* growing nicely in a moist, well-drained corner. It is a distinct and appealing character. Stems 1–3ft (30cm–1m) carry neat whorls of foliage and between one and perhaps ten horizontal or slightly downward-inclined clean-cut bells with sharp pointed tips widening but in no way reflexing. They have that distinctive bloom that seems to add so much mystery and quality to flowers, not that these need much extra adornment to their intriguing colours of rich wine or dark earthenware in bud and light crimson inside heavily spotted red. Toward the centre they become honey-coloured.

L. bolanderii is a rare plant in the wild, coming from restricted mountain homes in south Oregon and north California. *L. columbianum*, on the other hand, has a very wide distribution and has been found in habitats from the shoreline to over 5,000ft (1500m). From northern California it spreads through Oregon and is known from Idaho, up to Vancouver Island and British Columbia in Canada. It has the typical small turk's-cap flowers held very pendent on long ascending flower stalks from thin stems that reach from 2ft (60cm) to 5ft (1.5m). Open pyramids of some six to a dozen or more blooms are cheerful in tangerines more or less imbued with stronger orange and red. Normally it blooms a little later than the others of this series, in mid- to late summer.

From the Sierra Nevada of California hails the fine woodland lily, *L. humboldtii*, and the even more impressive and better tempered *L. ocellatum*, for long listed as a variety. The first species has pyramids of nodding turk's-caps each about 3in (7.5cm) across, in colour a showy orange, much spotted with maroon or aubergine. Petals from 2½in (6cm) to 4in (10cm) long recurve and point upward. A stem of 4–6ft (1–1.8m) is dramatic, with a dozen showy lanterns to a pyramid. *L. ocellatum* blossoms are a rich tangerine, but heavily ornamented with large spots of maroon, each spot likely to be ringed with crimson, the feature suggesting the specific name. The spots tend to run into one another around the tips, which thus become solidly painted red. It is much more strongly stem rooting than *L. humboldtii* and therefore is immediately more amenable to cultivation. In the wild it grows to the south and west of *L. humboldtii*, further proof of its separation from this species.

There is a group of small species that are rare in the wild and becoming rarer as the mounting pressures of development invade their homelands down the Pacific coastal lands of Oregon and California. *L. occidentale* is a small-bulbed rhizomatous lily with slender 2–5ft (60cm–1.5m) stems that carry hanging turk's-cap flowers of orange and crimson. *L. maritimum* is another small-flowering, dainty lily. Its shrinking habitat is low coastline bogs and well-watered meadows, where it may grow in association with scrub above the general level. Dark red flowers dotted with purple are formed of petals that try to maintain a funnel-shaped base but then in their last third curve out and back. *L. parvum* may be somewhat easier – it is a mountain species rather than a seaside *L. maritimum* type. It still enjoys getting its toes in moist soil though, because it grows on the edges of mountain streams and in meadows that are kept moist in the growing months by the melting snows higher up. The specific name refers to the flowers, which are delightful long bells swinging to the horizontal, or more upward. In colour they may be an unadulterated gold, but can be an alloy of gold and bronze-orange or red. The centres are neatly dotted maroon. Foliage may be scattered up the stem or may be whorled. The stems are not particularly 'parvum' – they will reach 3–5ft (90cm–1.5m).

Good drainage and gritty soil with generous helpings of leaf mould is recommended for the very fine *L. parryi* (see page 51). Some growers manage this well and amaze lesser mortals with stems of anything up to 6ft (2m) holding from one to perhaps more than two dozen outward-facing flowers whose basic funnel shape is disguised by the widely opening upper thirds of petals. All is rich gold with only minimal dark dotting. A pleasing scent is part of the package.

Neither the widespread *L. philadelphicum* or the little *L. catesbaei* are going to be widely grown garden plants unless new discoveries are made about their culture. *L. philadelphicum* grows only 2ft 6in–3ft (75–90cm) high and may have one to six wide-open, upward-facing flowers in almost any colour shadings from pale yellow to rusty oranges and deep venous blood reds. *L. catesbaei*, with tiny bulbs, has even less stem, with scattered thin leaves and probably only a single, wide-open, orange and gold flower. This will be spotted dark brown and have the petals so narrowly shafted at their base that one may look through the centre of the flower. A delicate, if intriguing, little dandy, it is one of the few lilies that maintain a rosette of leaves through the winter, not something that is to be recommended in poor climates.

Shortly after the New World was discovered, plants began to be sent back to Europe. One of the first to arrive was *L. canadense*, which the French brought back in 1620 and John Parkinson listed nine years later as 'the Spotted Martagon or Lilly of Canada'. Linnaeus gave this plant its present name in 1753. Although not generally reckoned to be difficult , certainly not by the standards of some of its fellow American species, it is never in much danger of getting out of control and becoming a nuisance.

Quality is stamped all over *L. canadense*. Stems rise some 2–5ft (60cm–1.5m) and are stylishly dressed with whorls of neat grass-green leaves augmented by a few scattered ones above the top whorl. Flowers are borne pendently, one to perhaps over twenty from a stem. Flower form is classic. Petals some 2–3in (5–8cm) long curve widely outward with the lower half but restrain any inclination to reflex above the horizontal, giving a most pleasing sculptured outline. In nature it is a widely distributed plant and there is a little, not too drastic, variation. Flower colour of cultivated forms is usually a clear shining lemon-gold, but it is possible to obtain orange ones. It is a plant of woodland margins and moister grasslands, which gives us a clue as to its culture. It can enjoy some shade, but will resent a heavy canopy, its bulbs like peaty moist soils but are the better for not being too swamped with winter wet. When all is well the bulbs will increase happily at a satisfying rate by pushing out stolons from parent bulbs, the ends of each stolon swelling to become a fresh bulb.

Botanically close to this last species is the very chic *L. grayi*, altogether rarer and more of a challenge to the cultivator. It has neat, whorled foliage and flowers of dark red, more orange inside, but held either horizontally or swinging upward close to this pose. There is variation in the shape of the blooms, the petals may like each other's company to the extent of making a narrow funnel only slightly opened at the end, but they may be rather less restrainedly tubular. Good drainage, plenty of peat, and ardent prayer would seem the only possible recommendations.

Again close botanically to *L. canadense*, but this time not a plant of outstanding difficulty, *L. superbum* (see page 54) can, indeed, be simply superb. Its flowers are pendent but the petals recurve quite strongly and the colour is usually orange with red tips so that one thinks perhaps of *L. pardalinum* rather than *L. canadense* as its immediate kin. It can be distinguished by the green flower centre made by the well-defined nectary furrows and also by the shape of the flat-sided buds, which are triangular in section. It is not a difficult garden plant, but it is, like *L. canadense*, a lime-hater, so if you have an irredeemably lime soil, you must rest content with *L. pardalinum*.

In the past the graceful *L. michiganense* has been mistaken for a hybrid between *L. canadense* and *L. superbum* and this may be a useful rough description of a widespread, perfectly good species. Green, clean stems some 2–5ft (60–150cm) high carry from one to over half a dozen delightfully posed flowers hanging from long upward and arching flower stalks. Petals curve back level with the stalks, their full orange well endowed with dark spots towards the bases. There are richer red forms as well as yellow ones. While bulbs are not often on offer, seed is not difficult to get. Bulbs appear to grow well in garden conditions and do not object to lime. *L. iridollae* is rarer with fewer blooms. Flowers are pendulous with recurving yellow petals decorated with much obvious brown spotting. It is unusual in producing basal leaves in the late summer, leaves that it retains over winter.

Candidum Group

These are the European species that were the only lilies known to gardeners before the discovery of the New World. To most people of this time, lily meant only *L. candidum* (see page 42), the madonna lily. This is an unusual lily in many ways. Like many kinds it is very vulnerable to virus diseases; when infected it deteriorates and is a threat to all other kinds nearby. It has the reputation of being a species that does better for the cottager than the expert. This is possibly because in a cottage garden it is well away from other lilies and is left undisturbed to get on with its life. Bulbs are best planted very shallowly with only a light covering of soil over their tops. After flowering in mid-summer it will produce a rosette of leaves at ground level and these mark its site through the winter. The wild forms found in the Balkans often have rather narrow petals, but cultivated selections are altogether more impressive, with crowded, outward-facing heads of gleaming white flowers.

Possibly nearest in appearance to *L. candidum* is *L. monadelphum*, with *L. szovitsianum*, which is now normally regarded as a subspecies. Bulbs are large, they are long lived and very hardy but may take a year to settle down as they resent disturbance. Stout stems have lots of scattered, light green leaves below heads of wide, hanging bells of yellow, usually a primrose shade but sometimes much paler or a fuller shade with a touch of burgundy at the base of the bud, and usually with a number of small purple spots drawn towards the edges of the petals – unlike most species, which tend to have their beauty spots gathered towards the base. As the blooms are large, petals being wide and about $3\frac{1}{2}$in (9cm) long, and as there may be half a dozen up to several times this number, they are very effective.

L. szovitsianum (see page 77) is better known in gardens and would appear to be the more ready of the two plants to grow, even naturalizing itself when left alone in conditions that suit it. Bulbs grow well if planted deeply in ordinary garden soils and do not mind the presence of lime. A soil covering of 5–7in (12–18cm) over the large bulbs would not be too much. I have known it to grow happily on very stiff London clay. Its natural habitat is in the margins of woods or in among a medley of vigorous thick-growing plants that keep its roots cool even while its top is basking in sunshine. The leafy stems may reach up to 5ft (1.5m) and may bear any number of flowers, from one to a splendid twenty in early summer. Hanging flowers have their $4\frac{1}{2}$in (10cm) petals spreading widely before curling back. The hanging anthers of rusty orange pollen contrast with the petals. Some forms come free of spots, but most have a few sprinkled in a column just in from the petal edges. Seed germinates freely, though it will be busy under the soil surface for a season before deigning to push leaves above. It will manage itself in the garden, if the seedlings are not harried and killed by constant hoeing.

European species such as *L. chalcedonicum*, *L. pomponium*, and *L. pyrenaicum* are related to the alpine species *L. carniolicum*, which has a distribution from northern Italy across to Romania, Hungary, and Yugoslavia. It is an attractive red-flowered turk's-cap, but a plant not at all common in cultivation. In the past it was somewhat eclipsed by the more brilliantly coloured, vivid scarlet *L. chalcedonicum* (see page 69), with its curled-up, polished blooms and more leafy stems. This species has now become a rarity although it still does well in a number of gardens.

L. pomponium is another brilliant, dark orange-red turk's-cap, this one marked with tiny black spots. It looks not unlike the more frequently cultivated *L. pumilum* from Asia. Although, in the wild it is rather frugal with flower, single ones being quite usual, in the garden the bulbs may produce half a dozen or more. It grows easily from seed. Flowers have a less than agreeable scent, something that the very useful early flowering *L. pyrenaicum* takes to further eccentric odoriferous lengths. Smell apart, *L. pyrenaicum* has everything going for it as a garden lily. It grows easily, it persists and increases on a diet of neglect, and it produces the earliest flowers of the genus in late spring and early summer. The flowers are a tight posy of hanging lemon-gold turk's-caps with plenty of dark freckles. So easy is the plant that it has spurned the confines of garden cultivation and gone into the wild in Devon. Like other Europeans, once planted it is best left to its own devices.

On its own in this group is the long-cultivated *L. bulbiferum* from the Pyrenees and the Alps. It has upward-facing flowers; from a narrow base the petals become wide and form attractive cups. Orange-red and yellow forms are found. The specific name refers to the plant's ability to produce bulbils in its leaf axils. Some individuals will do this freely with no stimulus needed, some will provide a lot one year and few the next, some will appear to be without bulbils but can be persuaded to give as good as the best by having their flowering tops lopped off early on.

Oriental Group

The horticultural stars of this group are *L. auratum* and *L. speciosum*, but all the species are beautiful plants. *L. rubellum* and *L. japonicum* stand halfway between our stars and the white Trumpet types *L. nobilissimum* and *L. brownii*.

L. speciosum is the most frequently seen, if only in florists' windows. Like the rest of its group, it suffers from the handicap of not liking lime. They have a simple expedient to deal with its presence – they die. However, given a neutral or somewhat acid soil, *L. speciosum* is as easy as any lily. It was introduced from its native Japan by the Dutch, who were virtually the only traders allowed into the closed Japan of those days. It arrived in Europe in 1830 and has been a favourite plant since then. Stock has been propagated in Europe, in America, and in the Antipodes, while new stock has been regularly imported from Japanese nurseries. One nurseryman, Mr Uchida, has made a speciality of it and rigorous reselection over many years has built up a very even and fine series bearing his name.

L. speciosum is useful in being a late-flowering kind. Under glass it responds well to forcing – commercial growers use it to provide blooms from early in the new year until the late autumn. Amateurs can grow it easily in pots. Slender, very wiry stems carry neat oval leaves on angled leaf stalks to make it a pleasing foliage plant before the buds appear. The well-spaced semi-pendent blooms are carried on long flower stalks in a posed style that seems to have real oriental grace. Petals sweep back to have their tips pointing heavenward, the white being suffused with crimson-pink and marked by unusual raised points, or papillae, that may or may not be marked with the dark crimson spotting that tends to decorate the base more heavily than the rest. Stems may have three to six blooms, but exceptional ones have been recorded with nearly fifty! There are pure white forms and others that have greater concentrations of the pink and crimson. All have a glorious scent. Outside they need plenty of humus, a cool root run, and excellent drainage. In gritty, leafy soils the stems will root strongly and for this reason the bulbs should be planted deeply.

The introduction of *L. auratum* (see page 43) was one of the great excitements of gardening history. It arrived in America and Europe in the early years of the 1860s and was instantly one of the wonders of the age. It remains a real wonder, with flowers 10–12in (25–30cm) across and standing anything from 3ft (1m) to 8ft (2.5m) high, with a modest five or six or up to a stupendous two or three dozen blooms. Each wide, flat, or shallow bowl-shaped star faces outward to make the most of its considerable beauty; the wide, white petals are banded gold in the centre (so earning the common name 'golden-rayed Japanese lily') and dotted with crimson. There are kinds in which the gold is replaced by crimson, which can invade most of the petal. *L. auratum* has one of the most powerful perfumes of any flower.

The Achilles' heel of this prodigy is its vulnerability to virus, which destroys it quickly. It is common sense, therefore, to grow this lily well clear of any obvious source of infection, any other lilies. It may be grown in pots. Bulbs need to be deeply planted in well-drained soil as it is a vigorous stem rooter. Indeed, a flourishing plant, when lifted at the end of the season can be revealed as a ruined bulb whose above-soil splendour has all been owed to the stem roots.

The lovely *L. japonicum*, with soft pink, trumpet-shaped, early summer flowers, is another joy when seen growing happily. Unfortunately it, too, is very virus-prone and it is not a rampant grower from bulbs, scales, or seeds. *L. rubellum* (see page 52) is another Japanese species, a dainty, very-early-blooming one with wonderful pink trumpets. It is like a dwarf version of the last, reaching only to 1ft 6in–3ft (45–90cm). It is initially difficult but if raised from seed it can become one of the gardener's proudest achievements. The rare white Trumpet *L. nobillisimum* is unusual in having flowers that are more or less upward looking. *L. brownii* is an outward-facing white Trumpet that is rare in cultivation and, although beautiful, perhaps eclipsed for garden use by easy-going kinds like *L. regale* and the hybrids.

Asian Group

The species within this group are an even more disparate lot than the others. They are scattered across the continent and, with the isolated *L. henryi* pivotally positioned, the rest may be conveniently divided into three lots – the tiger-lily types such as *L. lancifolium* and *L. davidii*, the rather smaller-flowered dainty kinds including *L. amabile*, *L. pumilum* and *L. cernuum*, and the third rather exotic ones that include rare kinds that approach the borderlines with the nomocharis together with larger unusual beauties like *L. nepalense*.

L. henryi (see page 41) is a mid-summer flower with sloping stems well clothed with neat, shiny, mid-green leaves. Blooms are largish, semi-pendent, tangerine-coloured, with petals curving back and making a feature of their papillae, a mass of long, pointed, fleshy eruptions. Stems, from 4ft (1.2m) to 8ft (2.4m), carry from a half dozen to over twenty flowers in their arching lengths. Exceptional stems can be longer and can carry even more flowers, over fifty is perfectly possible. While it grows well in full sun with a little shade around its base, it is best with some shade because the flowers fade in strong light. It should be given a position in which its strong stem roots can get to work. It does not object to lime and is a good doer; bulbs grow and split freely, bulblets are formed on the underground stems, and seed can be converted into flowering bulbs in three or four years. It is one of the easiest of all lilies to grow.

Perhaps nearest in appearance are *L. lancifolium* and *L. davidii*. Belonging with these are the less well-known *L. papilliferum*, *L. lankongense*, *L. duchartrei*, and *L. leichtlinii*. The tiger lily, *L. lancifolium* (see page 51), has many horticultural good points. Bulbs grow easily, flowers are attractive, the habit of the plant is fine, and the freedom with which it offers bulbils in its leaf axils is most satisfying. Against these points is the ease with which it will become virused and then continue growing with little apparent immediate effect but providing a very ready source of infection. It should be stationed well clear of other lilies. It has many pendent, rich orange blossoms with recurved petals generously spotted with purple-black. It stands 5–6ft (1.5–1.8m) tall.

L. davidii (see pages 106, 107) has flowers of rather similar colouring and shape, but the whole plant is somewhat more refined and a little smaller. It has similar dark foliage but narrower. Stems may carry up to as many as twenty blooms in a pyramid. Like the triploid forms of *L. lancifolium*, the bulbs are happy to grow in soils with some lime. It grows to 4–5 ft (1.2–1.5m).

L. leichtlinii (see page 70) looks like a tiger lily after an effective slimming course, but with spotted yellow flowers and well-clothed stems devoid of bulbils.

Unusual *L. papilliferum* is a rare little hill plant only some 1ft 6in (50cm) high and with turk's-caps of very dark maroon flowers. *L. lankongense* (see page 78) is a larger plant and one that has entered the breeding stakes by being one parent of a series of fine pendent Asiatic hybrids, notably those bred by Dr North. Its wiry stems carry plenty of dark narrow leaves and several well-spaced nodding flowers, perhaps a dozen or so in a pyramid, their recurved petals being pinky mauve with purple-red dots. They are scented. Bulbs grow well in deep soils on the acid side of neutral and with plenty of humus. *L. dachartrei* is a more slender relative. As grown in cultivation this is usually a dwarfish plant, the bulbs sending out stoloniferous stems on which in congenial conditions several new bulbs are formed. A normal height is 1–2ft (30–60cm), although in the wild it can grow to over 4ft (1.2m). Flowers are quite close to those of an albino martagon with a peppering of purple-maroon spots. It enjoys a gritty soil enhanced with leaf mould, and then, if happy, it will increase quickly and provide a good quota of stems each with a few blooms.

The *L. amabile*, *L. pumilum*, *L. cernuum*, *L. callosum* and *L. concolor* group of species is a series of dainty lilies not all that difficult to grow and increase. *L. amabile* is a vivid orange-red lily with nodding recurved blooms spotted black. It grows to 1ft 6in–3ft (45–90cm). It enjoys growing in association with other plants to keep its lower parts cool, that lowest part of the stem being more or less free from foliage, while anything up to eight or so flowers flaunt their brightness in the sunshine. It will stand considerable drought and still produce lots of bulblets on the underground stems. Bulbs are smallish and formed of a few relatively large scales. Seedlings grow easily and quickly.

This same quick reproduction from seed is a feature of the easy *L. pumilum* (*tenuifolium*) (see page 50) with its narrow spikes of curled, bright vermilion flowers on very wiry stems and its rather long, very narrow leaves. It will bloom from tiny bulbs no bigger than marbles, and this it does early on, perhaps not reaching above 1ft 6in (45cm) high. *L. cernuum* is very similar in dainty habit and general aspect, but its flowers are a mauve-pink. *L. callosum* is another similar lily, a later-flowering one, also easily raised from seed. Turk's-cap flowers are daintily posed on longish, ascending flower stalks, smallish but quite wide before the petals curl back on themselves. Colour is a dull dark red in bud but is a softer orange-red when open.

L. concolor (see page 45) is an unusual Asiatic in that it has upward-facing blossom. It is a delightful little lily for the garden and very tempting for cutting for the house. Slender stems are well clothed with long, narrow, pointed leaves and above are the wide stars of glistening red, either unadorned or with dark peppering in the centre. There is also a golden form. Stems reach 1ft–2ft 6in (30–75cm) and may have two or three stars or up to a dozen. It is not a difficult little bulb to grow but is not particularly long-lived so that it is wise to sow seed.

The last grouping of Asiatics to which we turn our attention includes the small plants from Yunnan and the high country of the north of Burma and surrounding states. *L. mackliniae* is delightful; it may be a narrow-leaved dwarf at 5–6in (12–15cm) or may grow to relatively giant stature at 2ft 6in (75cm). The nodding blooms are unusual for a lily – wide deep bells with petals overlapping most of their length and just slightly turning out at their tips.' Outside the flowers are a rosy mauve-purple, but inside they are white, just suffused with a suggestion of the outer colouring. Flowers measure 2in (5cm) across and are just as deep, large for the size of the plant and its character. *L. amoenum*, *L. sempervivoideum*, *L. sheriffiae* and *L. henricii* are all little species close to the Nomocharis genus, with pendent or semi-pendent bells of white, spotted or flushed with mauve-pink or purple.

L. taliense and *L. wardii* are rare species looking like Martagons with their pendent, recurved blooms. The first grows to some 4–6ft (1.2–1.8m) with white flowers much decorated with fine dots of purple. The second has a pink-mauve colour with purple dotting, the stems growing to 3–5ft (90–150cm).

Bulbs or seed of the species mentioned in the last two paragraphs are at present not in cultivation or are very scarce. Seed is however available of *L. nepalense* (see page 79). This is an elite lily with wide, sharply pointed leaves and hanging trumpets. These are narrow at the base but flare widely, with the petal tips turning upwards. *L. nepalense* comes from the central Himalayas and has an aura of strangeness about it. The colouring is a greeny lime-yellow, but with the major part of the inner petals down to the nectary a rich mahogany. It is a superb lily and if grown in a gritty leafy soil the stoloniferous stems should provide plenty of bulbous increase. *L. primulinum* is a closely related kind, but not so hardy or so early to bloom, its thick waxy flowers opening in late summer or autumn and being a yellowish green with their throats heavily overpainted a burgundy mahogany colour.

Trumpet Group

L. longiflorum the florist's Easter lily, is a very important commercial plant raised in millions for church decoration at the Easter festival and for weddings and funerals at other times. It is not as hardy as *L. regale* and so, in many temperate parts of the world, its use outside is limited. In warmer parts it is grown outside in gardens or as a cut flower. Its wide oval leaves and large white trumpets untouched by any dark colouring make an impressive plant. Buds may be somewhat greenish. It is very virus-prone. There are dwarf forms used for pot culture.

L. formosanum with beautiful narrow trumpets, has buds painted with burgundy but opens pure white, perhaps with a shadow of the outer colour discernible through the petals. This is hardier than is often thought; I have known it come through some very bad winters and still produce good stems of its attractive flowers later in the flowering year. This and a dwarf form can be one of the quickest to raise from seed to blooming plants. It can be managed in months.

L. wallichianum, from the forests of the Himalayas, is a refined long-trumpeted kind with the very slender form opening suddenly and widely at the mouth to measure at least 7in (18cm) across. A hint of green outside and in the base of the flower enhances its beauty.

L. philippinense outdoes all others in the slenderness of its trumpet form and its length. Inside the flowers are white as snow, outside they may be touched with green or wine.

L. neilgherrense has the distinction of being the species that grows closest to the equator; it hails from the hills of southern India, where it is now very rare. Flowers are massive, they can be from 7in (18cm) to an exceptional 12in (30cm) long. Creamy white outside and pure white within, but marked with gold to the base, these huge flowers are very impressive. Bulbs get into growth by sending the flower stems on a stoloniferous underground walkabout that may reach as far as 1–2ft (30–60cm) before turning up into daylight. However it does not object to being confined in a large pot.

There is no challenging the importance of *L. regale* (see page 44) as far as most gardeners are concerned. For them it is *the* white trumpet lily. Bulbs grow strongly from seed and eventually stems are capable of carrying from one to as many as thirty of the large, wine-coloured buds that open to reveal sparkling white interiors with throats gilded. The whole is enveloped in a cloud of perfume. The ever-present problem with virus can be kept at bay by raising fresh batches of bulbs from seed. In two seasons many will be ready to bloom, given decent culture all will be flowering size in three.

The species *L. sargentiae*, a prolific bulbil producer, blooms a little later in the year, bearing a flower similar to that of *L. regale*. Less hardy than *L. regale*, this elegant species may need the protection of glass. *L. leucanthum* is a green-stemmed, leafy plant with ivory white flowers with throats usually somewhat yellowed, the outside of the petals being either creamy white or with a green line down their centres. In gardens its value is less than some of the hybrid races that have been bred from it. *L. sulphureum* is one of the gems of the genus, a strong but late-flowering lily that produces bulbils in the leaf axils. Flowers are of refined trumpet shape, not too widely expanded at the mouth, and of yellow colouring. The strength of the yellow varies. It grows outside to some 5–8ft (1.5–2.5m) but will outdo this under glass. As it blooms in the late summer or even well into the autumn, in colder areas it requires protective care. It is not widespread in cultivation but there are some virus-free stocks that hopefully can be maintained and increased. It looks well and has an intoxicating perfume.

HYBRID LILIES

It is the hybrid lilies that have changed the character of the genus as far as the amateur gardener is concerned. Their increasing diversity and sheer numbers have widened the choice available, but it is the greater ease of culture that has brought the lily from being the plaything of the dedicated few and of the rich with their squad of professional gardeners, to being a plant for everybody. This has happened mainly in the past four decades.

Classification of Hybrids

Assessing the relationships between wild plants and arranging a working classification can never be entirely satisfactory and never be final.

With the arrangement of the increasing numbers of hybrids the approach is entirely more pragmatic. While it is certainly possible to mirror much of the format of the species classification, the expansion of the hybrid races needs a somewhat different approach. The flow of new kinds means that it is desirable to keep a watching brief so that, if need arises, some adaptation of the accepted grid may be agreed. At present the garden classification is proving perfectly adequate. Its increased use by nurserymen and traders will help to ensure its wider acceptance by gardeners and a greater comprehension of catalogues and shows.

1 Asiastic. Cultivars bred from species such as *L. amabile*, *L. bulbiferum*, *L. cernuum*, *L. concolor*, *L. dauricum*, *L. davidii*, *L. lancifolium*, *L. lankongense*, *L. leichtlinii*, *L. maximowiczii* and *L. pumilum* together with the early hybrid races *L.* × *maculatum*, and *L.* × *hollandicum*.

This is by far the largest division, the one that houses most of the cultivars used extensively as cut flowers and pot plants as well as exciting border characters. To make it somewhat more manageable it is split into three sections depending on the pose of the flowers. So we get the subdivisions:

1A Upward-facing flowers. These are normally early summer flowers of firm, upright habit and usually about 2ft 6in (75cm) high. Example, 'Enchantment'.
1B Outward-facing flowers. These are also early flowers of similar habit to 1A. Example, 'Brandywine'.
1C Downward-facing flowers. These are normally just a little later to open than the foregoing. Examples, the Citronella strain and most North hybrids.

2 Martagon. Cultivars with one of the martagons as parent, or derived from such hybrids. Example, the Backhouse hybrids.
3 Candidum. Cultivars derived from *L. candidum* or other European species, excluding *L. martagon*. Example, *L.* × *testaceum*.
4 American. Cultivars derived from the crossing of members of the American group species. Example, 'Shuksan'.
5 Longiflorum. Cultivars derived from members of the *L. longiflorum* Trumpet species.
6 Trumpet. Cultivars derived from other Trumpet species, such as *L. leucantheum*, *L. regale*, *L. sargentiae* and *L. sulphureum*, together with Asian types such as *L. henryi*, but excepting the Orientals. These are divided into four sections:

6A Trumpet-shaped flowers. Example, Pink Perfection.
6B Bowl-shaped, outward-facing flowers. Examples, Heart's Desire strain, 'New Era'.
6C Pendent flowers.
6D Star-shaped flowers. Examples, the Sunburst series, 'White Henryi'.

7 Oriental. Cultivars derived from Oriental group species such as *L. auratum*, *L. japonicum*, *L. rubellum* and *L. speciosum*, including any hybrids between these and *L. henryi*. There are four sections:

7A Trumpet-shaped flowers.
7B Bowl-shaped flowers.
7C Flat-faced flowers. Examples, 'Stargazer', the Imperial series.
7D Recurved flowers. Example, 'Journey's End'.

8 Miscellaneous. Cultivars that do not fall into any other division.

The Development of Hybrids

Today's hybrids can be used in a variety of ways. With the shrinking size of the average garden and the increased interest in patio gardening, lilies in pots and containers have come into their own. Because the early-flowering Asiatic hybrids are so easy to manage in pots they have been the main beneficiaries of this shift of interest, but more and more Trumpet and Oriental kinds are being potted up. All these kinds are also finding increased representation in mixed beds and borders. The most has to be made of limited space, and lilies, giving so much in relatively small areas and delighting in growing in association with other plants, are ideal for this purpose. They bloom when the garden is at its most interesting and in the most accessible months. Those hoping to create something closer to the wild but still giving plenty of colour and interest, find in the Martagon and American hybrids just what is needed.

It would seem that the earliest Japanese lilies of mixed parentage were the upright-facing kinds, probably bred from *L. dauricum*, *L. wilsonii*, and other species, perhaps in the first place as the result of accidental cross-pollination. It was once thought that *L. concolor* was much involved but cytological examination has proved this to be incorrect. In about 1830 bulbs of some of these hybrids were brought to Holland under the name *L. maculatum* and established there and, with the dissemination of the hybrids, it was not long before the raising of improved kinds, especially of the Asiatic group, was well under way in Europe and America. One successful breeder was a London nurseryman, Henry Groom, who wrote: 'I crossed *L. bulbiferum* with *L. maculatum atrosanguineum* and have obtained some beautiful varieties, most having very brilliant colours and many being finely blotched with the deep colour of *L. atrosanguineum*.'

An accidental hybrid in Germany early in the 1800s indicated how dramatic the new lilies might be. The Asiatic hybrids, although attractive and useful, became almost predictable once the idea of crossing rather similar species had been born. The German hybrid was something altogether different. It was born of the two distinct species *L. candidum* and *L. chalcedonicum*. It must have caused huge excitement arriving unannounced and unexpected in the middle of a bed of lilies. Happily the hybrid inherited the persistent longevity of the parents and, although eventually falling victim to virus, it has persisted. Tissue culture has been used to eliminate the disease and make available clean bulbs. The cross has been repeated and the hybrid back-crossed with its parents to provide a range of very pleasing plants, all easy to grow and happy in gardens with limey soils.

The introduction in the 1860s of the fantastic *L. auratum* to join the earlier arrival *L. speciosum* (1830), stimulated the imagination of more than one grower. In the United States, Francis Parkman, a distinguished historian who had retraced the old Oregon Trail westward from St Louis, produced a hybrid named 'Parkmannii'. His original attempt at the cross had failed. A second try resulted in around fifty seedlings. All except one bloomed identically with the mother, *L. speciosum*; the odd one was 'Parkmannii', which was shown in London in 1875. Later on it succumbed to the virus diseases that are a constant threat to Oriental hybrids.

Quite different was the result of interbreeding the species *L. martagon* and *L. hansonii*. Several growers saw the possibilities in this cross and began to raise plants. In particular, Mrs R. O. Backhouse carried on the work over a long period, beginning in the 1890s. Her hybrids are still grown today.

A batch of seed of hybridized American species grown on by Dr David Griffiths of the United States Department of Agriculture laid the basis of the Bellingham hybrid strain of lilies.

By the second half of the 1920s the idea of large-scale lily hybridization took hold in the United States, in Australia, and in New Zealand, as well as in Europe. Amateur and professional growers all over the world started to work rather more systematically. The largest operation of all undertaken to breed new lilies was that initiated by Jan de Graaff at his Oregon Bulb Farms (see page 15); bulbs from this source were distributed worldwide and hugely changed the gardener's attitude to the lily. The highly successful Mid-Century series not only successfully invaded our gardens but gained the interest of professional growers of bulbs and cut flowers. 'Enchantment', one of the first of these Mid-Century lilies, virtually founded an industry which has continued and expanded.

Asiatic Hybrids

The Asiatics were the first lilies to be cross-bred and more Asiatics than any other lilies are grown today, in home gardens and commercially. An indication of how lily cultivation has expanded is the acreage being grown in Holland. In 1987 the most-grown lily was 'Connecticut King' with some 560 acres (227 ha). The former top favourite, 'Enchantment' was grown on about 476 acres (193 ha). The third most-grown kind was the Oriental 'Stargazer', with about 454 acres (184 ha). Of the next seven in order of popularity, six were Asiatics – 'Sunray', 'Uchida', 'Yellow Blaze', 'Sterling Star', 'Esther', 'Roma', and 'Yellow Giant'.

The first Japanese hybrids imported into Europe in the 1830s were plants between 1ft (30cm) and 2ft (60cm) tall, with upward-facing flowers that could be any colour from lemon to a deep red. They were vegetatively reproduced in Holland under the name *L. maculatum*, with different clones being given botanical varietal names. One well-known selection was 'Alice Wilson', a clear lemon yellow with dark red spots, which was named after the daughter of G. F. Wilson, whose home and garden became the foundation of the Royal Horticultural Society's gardens at Wisley. Given a First Class Certificate by the Royal Horticultural Society in 1877, it was still being grown when Jan de Graaff started his work.

While most of the species involved in the Asiatic breeding programme were, of course, from Asia, one European species made a very significant contribution. This gate-crasher was *L. bulbiferum*. *L. × maculatum × L. bulbiferum* gave a series of plants known collectively as *L. × hollandicum*. They had good polished foliage, stouter stems, reaching 1ft 6in–2ft 6in (45–75cm) high, and firmly held, upright flowers of as wide a colour spectrum as the maculatums but of improved intensity. These were distributed all over the world and were widely acclaimed.

Early breeding was bedevilled by the pseudoscientific names given to some hybrids. In the 1930s J. E. H. Stooke, working in Herefordshire, gave the names 'Cromottiae' and 'Crovidii' to two seedlings that resulted from crossing *L. bulbifernum croceum* with *L. davidii willmottiae*. Nonetheless, many of Stooke's hybrids were useful and some are still grown today. His 'Fire King' is a vigorous lily with many outward-facing wide flowers crowded on stems up to 4ft (1.2m) tall. It is a deep red, spotted with purple.

At the Boyce-Thompson Institute for Plant Research in New York State flowers of *L. × hollandicum* clones were crossed with a fresh species, *L. lancifolium*, and the progeny named 'Umbtig', the idea being to combine the first syllables of the parents' names, *umbellatum* being a now-discontinued synonym for *hollandicum* and 'tig' being from *L. tigrinum*, now more correctly called *L. lancifolium*. The seedlings grew to about 3ft (90cm) and had well-spaced, wide leaves held at right angles to the stems. Flowers were upright but were wider and a little shallower than those of previous series and were displayed in broad, ample umbels, the colours ranging from amber to fiery reds decorated with maroon spots.

Jan de Graaff took the Umbtig series as seed parents and crossed them with the old maculatum 'Alice Wilson'. This was the basic cross of the Mid-Century hybrids. Although the Martagon and Bellingham hybrids had been accepted widely as garden plants, it was with the introduction of the very easily mass-propagated Mid-Centuries that the lily became a popular garden plant for everyone. Outstanding cultivars included:

Cinnabar Bred from 'Fireflame' × *L. hollandicum*, this is a sturdy plant with well-spaced dark maroon flowers of pointed petals, the bases of which are peppered with dark dots. Height 2ft (60cm).

Enchantment This (see page 33) is the most famous of all lily hybrids. Since its introduction forty years ago it has been grown in astronomical numbers as a garden plant, as a pot lily, and as a cut flower. Strong stems of clean, pointed foliage support heads of flaming fluorescent orange flowers. There may be any number up to twenty in a wide, closely arranged head. Petals reach out and curve back. 'Enchantment' grows strongly, increases with consummate ease, and is altogether a very worthwhile character. Height 2–3ft (60–90cm).

Fireflame Brilliant vermilion flowers with a little spotting. Height 2ft–2ft 6in (60–80cm).

Harmony With rather fewer flowers to a head than some but with wider petals than most, 'Harmony' is an engaging soft amber-orange not very much disturbed by a few small dark spots. It is stout-stemmed and shorter than some. Good in pots. Height 1ft 6in–2ft 6in (45–75cm).

Tabasco Bred from 'Fireflame' × *L. hollandicum*, it has rich chestnut-red flowers only lightly dotted with black, each being well formed of pointed, widespread petals, the whole head having a brooding rich colour. Dark stems with narrow leaves arching downward. Height 2–4ft (60–120cm).

Valencia This differs from the above in facing outward rather than up and the colours are a palish tangerine with a darker midrib and a more golden centre with small purple spots. Height 3ft (90 cm).

The main lily species so far represented in the genetic stew of hybridization are *L. dauricum*, *L. wilsonii*, *L. bulbiferum*, and *L. lancifolium*. The next step was to introduce the blood of *L. davidii*, in the hope of using its free-flowering habit, its pyramidal arrangement, its brilliant orange-reds, its turk's-cap form, and its pendent pose. A number of breeders had worked this seam, notably Isabella Preston in Ottawa, Canada, who used the *L. dauricum* and *L.* × *maculatum* hybrids to interbreed with *L. davidii* to produce the Stenographer hybrids. The most successful Stenographers were the brilliant red, outward-looking 'Brenda Watts' and 'Lillian Cummings', a pendent, vibrant red kind with dark spots and purple-painted petal bases.

De Graaff cultivars resulting from the mating of Mid-Century types with *L. davidii* included:

Joan Evans With rich, golden-tangerine flowers and broad petals dotted maroon, this is a vigorous lily, a little taller and later than the first Mid-Centuries. Heads of six to nine blooms. Height 3ft–3ft 6in (90–105cm).

Paprika An outward-looking, thick-substanced lily of glowing crimson. Height 2–3ft (60–90cm).

Other species were also used. The yellow form of *L. amabile* for example, was crossed with the Mid-Centuries to give fine yellow hybrids; the best are:

Croesus Wide goblets of amber gold have a few dark spots toward the centre. Sturdy stems hold thick-substanced flowers. Height 3ft (90cm).

Destiny From *L. amabile luteum* × 'Valencia'. Bulbs with many narrow scales produce strong, wiry, dark stems with neat foliage and well-arranged heads of wide, bright lemon-gold blooms generously spotted in the centre, petal tips turn downward. Height 3–4 ft (90–120cm).

Prosperity Although of the same parentage as 'Destiny', 'Prosperity' is unlike its sibling in having flowers facing outward. Otherwise the two varieties are not dissimilar. 'Prosperity' has slightly less heavily spotted lemon-gold petals. It has dark stems and rich, healthy leaves. Height 3ft (90cm).

Later developments of the Preston hybrids produced flowers of upward, outward, and downward poses and of many colours, including good yellows. De Graaff took the best of these and mated them with *L. amabile* to produce the Fiesta hybrids. Bulbs of these were distributed in mixed lots, or as colour strains. They are still grown and offered. They are basically mid-summer flowers, taller than most Mid-Centuries and with pendent pose. They were the first important Asiatic hybrids with hanging flowers. Of these older strains still available today, the most significant are:

Bronzino Mid-summer flowers in a variety of shades and combinations of colours including warm ambers, flushed golds, and oranges, heavily imbued with richer hues of mahogany and chocolate. Height 3–5ft (90–150cm).

Burgundy These are similarly prolific, with up to a score of flowers on strong stems, the colours being mostly rich wine shades, clarets, and burgundies, but with some varieties more cherry coloured. Height 3–5ft (90–150cm).

Citronella These lilies (see page 67), perhaps the best liked of the Fiestas by gardeners, have lemon-gold flowers with petals curling back and attractively spotted with purple-black. Long pyramids carry very many flowers, which vary in size according to the clone. Some are quite large, but even the smallest are impressive because so many are produced on the spikes. They can hold their own in competition with more modern hybrids. Height 3–4ft (90–120cm).

The use of *L. cernuum* in breeding programmes further defeated the dominant upward-facing habit of most Asiatic hybrids. Dr Patterson, at the Department of Horticulture of Saskatchewan University, had been breeding from *L. lancifolium* and the *L. davidii* hybrid 'Maxwill'. To them he added the mauve-pink *L. cernuum* to raise a very wide range of flowers, more-or-less hanging, and having many pastel shades from creams to pinks and salmons. Some were grown as named clones, and outstanding among these were 'Lemon Queen', 'Rose Queen', and 'White Princess'. Two of his raising became important in subsequent breeding programmes.

Lemon Queen This was bred from one of the Stenographer series, 'Grace Marshall', by a seedling. It was a very prolific bloomer with perhaps two or three dozen rich lemon, outward-looking flowers with reflexed petals to a stem.

Edith Cecilia From a light-flowered seedling of *L. davidii*, this had hanging orange-buff flowers with richer petal tips.

It may have been the same seedling from 'Lemon Queen' crossed with 'Edith Cecilia' that gave a series of seedlings that included 'Discovery' and 'Corsage' – or, since 'Corsage' was introduced in 1961, five years before 'Discovery', perhaps the parentage was similar but not

133

identical. 'Corsage' has been grown since as one of a very few hybrids that have produced good plants and fine flowers but have had atrophied anthers. No pollen at all is produced and so the flowers are singularly well suited for corsages, hence the name.

Corsage Although not one of the largest-flowered hybrids, it produces plenty of outward-facing, widely opened and reflexing blooms of interesting pale pastel colours. The centre is a pale creamy primrose merging to rosy pink at the petal tips, this pink being evident in the buds. The centres are boldly flecked with dark maroon spots.

Discovery This (see page 87) was bred from a lily with the parentage 'Lemon Queen' × 'Mega', crossed with 'Edith Cecilia', a Patterson seedling from *L. davidii*. 'Mega' was a lemon seedling from the Stenographer clone 'Brenda Watts'. Flowers of long, outward-pointing petals are an unusual dusky shade of rich rosy lilac but with a paler base, a white suffused with pink and dotted dark crimson. The colour is concentrated in the petal tips.

Lilies with the same parents as 'Discovery' were used as seed parents for a number of Mid-Century hybrids and through them an important new generation of plants was raised.

Chinook With 'Enchantment' as father 'Chinook' was introduced in 1972 and is still going strong. It has tall stems, perhaps 4ft (1.2m) high with many well-spaced upward-and-outward looking medium-sized flowers of buff-apricot.

Sterling Star This cultivar (see page 88) belongs to the generation of hybrids that gave a number of fine white Asiatics. 'Sterling Star' has 'Discovery' or a plant of similar breeding as seed parent, with the yellow 'Croesus' as its Mid-Century father. It has proved one of the most successful commercial lilies since its introduction in 1973. Wiry dark stems with dark narrow leaves hold a widely spaced head of white stars facing the sky, the petals decorated by a generous scattering of dark spots in their lower halves.

Medaillon Of unknown parents 'Medaillon' is another cool-coloured flower but with much wider petals, creamy coloured with a central blotch of gold. It is stockier, with broader leaves, than 'Sterling Star'.

At Oregon, Mid-Centuries were crossed with *L. cernuum*. Selections of the resulting progeny were marketed as the Harlequin strain. Harlequin lilies include a wide range of shades from ivories to salmons, golds, and mixed pinks and yellows. The flowers are outward looking or semi-pendent and are characterized by wide-swept, recurving petals with much-freckled centres.

L. cernuum made possible a widening of the Asiatic lily colour spectrum, with more pink and mauve flowers appearing. Because of their parentage, the plants tended to have rather narrow leaves and wiry stems.

Rosita This came from an Asiatic hybrid crossed by *L. cernuum*. It bears pleasing open flowers that look upward and have widespread petals of lilac toned with rosy pink. The buds are pale, the foliage and stems dark. It has uncrowded heads of blossom.

Liberation The parentage is uncertain but 'Liberation' probably has some cernuum blood. It is distinct from 'Rosita' in having blooms in a more pyramidical arrangement that face outward and upward. Long, pointed petals recurve gracefully and are coloured a glowing rich pink-mauve with a few small dots in the base.

Zephyr *L. cernuum* features strongly in the background breeding of this lily. It is a sophisticated character with a pleasing relaxed demeanour. Smooth, wide-open, upward-looking flowers are of a soft rose-pink, with a scatter of small beauty spots.

Exception This also has much *L. cernuum* blood mixed with that of *L. davidii*. Like 'Corsage' it has no pollen, but the colour is distinct. Many medium-sized flowers face outward; they have pale lemonade centres but are a very dark maroon made more telling by a high-gloss finish. The anthers are reduced to the likeness of tiny flattened petals.

New hybrids are launched each season. At present some of the loveliest are those with pink colouring.

Corsica This has long, pointed petals with a lilac-shaded pink giving way to light ivory cream toward the centre but with a much darker, reddish-pink throat, this darker colour taken outward by the nectaries. Upward-facing flowers have a few small, dark pink dots in a band around the throat. Height 2ft (60cm).

Crete Uniformly coloured rich wine-pink flowers with long pointed petals make pleasing upward-facing heads of long-lasting flowers. It is one of the deepest of this colouring so far and is without any spotting. Height 2–3ft (60–90cm).

A new addition to the genetic input of the Asiatics was made by introducing *L. lankongense*. The most important of these were bred by Dr North at the Scottish Horticultural Research Institute at Invergowrie. His work resulted in a series of hybrids with tall pyramids of more-or-less pendent flowers with recurving petals. Colours are wide ranging, most being a blend of several pastel shades, all very bewitching. These lilies are usually scented, a feature absent in the other Asiatic hybrids. Some leading cultivars are:

Angela North Well-spaced recurved blooms hang in tall pyramids, displaying their rich, deep pink colours and dispensing scent.

Ariadne From *L. lankongense* × 'Maxwill'. Individual flowers are made of curled-back petals whose tips may touch the flower stalks that hold the very pendent blooms well spaced in tall, narrow pyramids. The hanging appearance is exaggerated by the long, downward-pointing style and hanging dark anthers. The colours of the flowers are a lovely mix of very pale pink-orange with a richer mauve-pink to the centre of each petal and with plenty of rusty maroon spots. Long, hanging buds are flushed with pastel orange shades.

Barbara North Tall, narrow pyramids with lots of hanging flowers of good rich pink.

Eros The seed parent of 'Eros' was bred from *L. lankongense* crossed by *L. davidii*. The Asiatic father is recorded as having the blood of many things in it – Citronella, 'Destiny', 'Redbird', and *L. lancifolium flaviflorum*. It looks a typical North hybrid with very recurved, wide, pendent blooms. It is less tall than some at 3–4 ft (90–120cm). Painted in shades of pink with a sprinkling of dark spots.

Iona This (see page 92) has larger flowers than some of the other *L. lankongense* hybrids, and these are painted in shades of glowing coral pinks.

Marie North A stylish hybrid with a pyramid of blossom, effective dark buds, and well-reflexed, opened blooms basically white but lightly suffused with a suggestion of blush pink.

Peggy North A vigorous hybrid (see page 93) with turk's-cap flowers and stronger colours than most of its relatives – a rich, warm orange with spots.

Rosemary North Another delightful, pastel-coloured hybrid, an amalgam of muted orange and buff.

Theseus A robust, scented, triploid hybrid that carries impressively thick-textured, deep red flowers with petals swept back in a perfect arc and prominent orange-pollened anthers. The buds are richly coloured.

New departures are being made on other fronts. One involves the use of the old Russian hybrid 'Fialkovaya', bred from *L. szovitsianum* crossed with a maculatum clone. *L. szovitsianaum* is now usually regarded as a subspecies of *L. monadelphum* so that the range of hybrids, some introduced as Faberge hybrids, may have their breeding attributed in catalogues to *L. monadelphum*. 'Fialkovaya' has rosy lilac flowers with yellow centres; the hybrids are mainly pink and outward facing. At present they are being offered as a mixed strain but a few clones have been selected and named. *L. monadelphum* is a hardy long-living lily, but one that does not like being moved; the hybrids retain some of this dislike of disturbance and take a little while to fully settle. Small bulbs raised from tissue culture will settle more quickly than full-sized bulbs. They enjoy lime in the soil and are plants that will do well in climates that have cold winters and hot summers. They are early-flowering kinds.

Gipsy Queen Wide flowers, much of the *L. monadelphum* form, are outward or slightly downward looking. Right in the throat the colour is a dark red but this gives way to a creamy yellow throat but with the major proportion of the petals a rich red. There are a few dark spots scattered in the centre. It is one of the earliest of the larger-flowered lilies. Height 3–4ft (90–120cm).

Nutcracker This is an upward-facing hybrid with pointed-petalled blooms of rich raspberry-pink enhanced with cream centres that have decorative crimson spots. Well spaced dark-anthered blooms look very refined. Height 3–4ft (90–120cm).

L. pumilum has tantalized breeders for many decades. As with a number of other species, when foreign pollen is applied to its stigmas the plant looks to have accepted it as the pods swell, but the seed is normally pure *L. pumilum*. However, occasionally genuine hybrids are raised. 'Scamp' was raised in the 1960s from the species crossed with a Golden Chalice seedling. Judith McRae and Len Marshall have worked with *L. pumilum* and other species trying to incorporate new blood into the Asiatics. *L. pumilum* was successfully crossed with a bicolor Rainbow hybrid and the seedling selfed to give a range of interesting lilies. 'Red Carpet' was one very strong kind to come out of the cross, a plant with good disease resistance, something that had been in the minds of breeders working this area. 'Viva' was another strong kind, but this time from *L. pumilum* × *L. leichtlinii maximowiczii* and later flowering than most. At present some of the leading lilies with some *L. pumilum* blood are:

Cabriole This has both *L. pumilum* and *L. davidii* in the background of its breeding, making it a good garden plant. Its gracefully held, hanging flowers are a soft peach-fawn colour, unspotted, but with a touch of green towards the nectaries. It is a useful breeding plant. Height 2–3ft (60–90cm).

Doeskin From the *L. pumilum* seedling, 'Albipayne', by the robust 'Connecticut King', this has become a favourite with those that grow it for show or for the garden. It makes neat pyramid heads of many hanging flowers very well-placed. Petals recurve to show off the creamy buff unspotted colour tones that are beautifully contrasted with the red pollen. A strong plant that increases quickly and blooms in June. Height 2–3ft (60–90cm).

Fiery Sunset This is a rich orange-red turk's-cap kind with up to three dozen pendent blooms to a stem. It can be bred to give strong plants with similarly coloured flowers. Height 3–4ft (60–120cm).

Silverspring This is an outstanding addition to the pumilum Asiatics. With many flowers well-spaced, it shines pure white with, toward the centres, sprinkles of narrow pink dots. Pose is outward or downward and it has a long succession of bloom. Height 3ft (90cm).

Red Snappers This is a new strain with a complicated breeding background involving the species *L. cernuum*, *L. concolor*, *L. davidii* and *L. pumilum*. They do retain the feel of the species, with lots of gracefully-held, pendent, turk's-cap flowers on long heads retained for some weeks. Colouring covers the rich part of the spectrum involving deep scarlets to darker wine shades. Height 3ft (90cm).

Martagon Hybrids

The distinct character of these hybrids comes from the combined inheritance of the widespread *L. martagon* and the robust *L. hansonii*. The cross was made between these two species using a dark martagon, *L. martagon dalmaticum*, in Holland in the last century. The result was the *dalhansonii* hybrids. While both the parent species are very worthy, long-lived garden plants, the hybrids are better value and have a wider range of interesting colours. The petals of *L. hansonii* are only slightly reflexed and point away from the flower, those of the martagon curl into balls. The hybrids effect a sensible and attractive compromise between the two forms.

Marhan This (see page 59) was the result of crossing *L. martagon album* with *L. hansonii* and was bred by the famous Dutch firm of Van Tubergen and introduced in 1891. It is an exceptionally fine, strong plant with a narrow column of hanging or slightly outward-facing flowers with petals strongly recurving, nearly as markedly as those of the martagon. In bud the colour is a mauve-pink with perhaps a little gold and chocolate spotting peeping through the petal edges. The tawny rich gold of the flowers is enriched with plenty of chocolate spots. Petal tips of young flowers are overlaid with mauve, but this fades in sunlight to leave a paler blotch.

A series of hybrids was bred in England, at Sutton Court near Hereford, by the Backhouse family from the 1890s until the 1920s. Various colour forms of *L. martagon* were used with *L. hansonii*. There are still stands of these hybrids growing at Sutton Court today, although much of the time since the 1920s they have had to look after themselves. Most of the cultivars recommended below are kinds with the petals widespread and somewhat reflexed but not recurving on themselves.

Sutton Court This (see page 53) is similar in colour to 'Marhan', perhaps fractionally paler. The petals do not recurve so much as do those of many Backhouse hybrids.

Dairy Maid The creamy yellow flower is much spotted with chocolate-maroon, especially toward the centre.

Early Bird One of the first to open, with tangerine flowers lightly spotted and with suffused pink in the petal tips, especially in bud – the pink fades in open flowers.

Indian Chief A copper-coloured sport from 'Marhan', having the same turk's-cap flowers.

Mrs R. O. Backhouse Rich, glossy, tangerine-coloured blooms are flushed with gold and spotted dark red.

Shantung A pinky-mauve, lightly spotted, tall selection closer to its martagon parent than most.

W. O. Backhouse A second-generation hybrid, it has deep orange, heavily spotted, moderately reflexed flowers.

Paisley hybrids were raised in Oregon from all the flowers of this group, but mainly from *L. martagon album* and *L. hansonii*. Between them they have all the colours of a Paisley shawl.

Rarer related species, *L. tsingtauense* and *L. medeoloides*, have more recently been used by a few amateurs in the breeding of Martagon hybrids. The difficulty about all these attractive Martagon lilies is that they are slow to propagate – from seed they may take five to seven years to reach flowering size and they are scarcely quicker from scales. Commercial growers, conscious of profit margins, find other types easier, quicker, and more remunerative.

Candidum Hybrids

This is at present only a very small group of lilies, and the majority of these are the work of a few keen amateur growers. There is one notable exception. This is a hybrid between *L. candidum* and *L. chalcedonicum* that turned up by chance in a German garden nearly two centuries ago. The parents are totally dissimilar – the madonna lily with wide, outward-facing, white flowers packed close to the stem and *L. chalcedonicum*, with tightly curled, very pendent, shining red turk's-caps. *L. × testaceum* is midway between these extremes. The apricot-yellow flowers hang and are very wide with petals curving back. The plant was widely grown and became virus infected, but some stock has been cleaned up so that it may be purchased again. It stands 4–5ft (1.2–1.5m) tall, its heads carry several large, wide flowers. The cross has been repeated and *L. × testaceum* itself has been back-crossed with *L. candidum*, all with very pleasing results.

A new departure has led to the introduction of Asiatic blood into this group. Judith McRae managed to raise seedlings using embryo culture technique. A few clones have been named.

Uprising A strong growing kind with tall, very dark stems and long flower stalks. Wide flowers are of soft yellow and cream with a light scatter of dark spots. Height 5ft (1.5m).

Limerick Hanging or slightly outward-facing blooms have a graceful pose and are a lovely soft lime-coloured tone. Height 3–4ft (90–120cm).

American Hybrids

In America lilies are found growing wild from the east to the west coast, but it is the rather more horticulturally amenable ones from the Pacific coast that have given rise to the best garden hybrids. These are tall, mid-summer lilies with erect stems holding bold, whorled foliage and turk's-cap flowers – like the Martagon's but much larger and not usually so severely curled back on themselves. A large amount of hybrid seed was sown by Dr David Griffiths of the United States Department of Agriculture in 1919. The resulting seedlings, first marketed in 1932 as the Bellingham hybrids, proved easier to grow than any of the parents. Flower colours range from all yellow through yellow and red to virtually all red, with greater or lesser degrees of dark dotting.

The species involved in the breeding of the original series were *L. pardalinum* × *L. ocellatum* and *L. parryi* × *L. ocelatum*, but those with *L. pardalinum* blood became the more dominant through their greater size and vigour. Later the blood of other Americans was introduced, such as *L. bolanderii* and *L. kelloggii*. A few clones were isolated and given names and have since become popular garden plants.

Buttercup This 1954 selection has good-sized, reflexed flowers in shining deep gold well endowed with bold spots.

Shuksan Selected as long ago as 1933, this (see page 95) is believed to be a *L. humboldtii* × *L. pardalinum* hybrid. With a good record of garden performance, 'Shuksan' is probably the best known of this group. It stands 4–6ft (1.2–1.8m) and has rounded flowers of rich tangerine-gold, lightly spotted. The upward-pointing petal tips are rich crimson.

More recently Derek Fox in England has worked with these flowers and introduced some very lovely kinds that are clear leaders in the group:

Lake Tahoe The long, narrow petals sweep out and upward from a white centre. More than half of the upper petal is painted a rich pink, while the base has a touch of yellow and a small green centre.

Lake Tulare This is similar, with maroon-pink petals shading down to a white centre and spotted deep crimson. The flowers are held well spaced on longish stalks, each bloom hanging gracefully but with its long petals pointing upward.

The Bullwood hybrids are from *L. pardalinum* × a pink 'Henry Bolander' hybrid. These are clean-cut, beautifully posed, pendent flowers in many shades of gold, apricot, red, and cherry. Some of the most effective are those with a lot of this cherry-red colouring, a shade distinct from the more usual, harsher orange-reds of most Bellinghams. They are characterized by the good size of the flowers, which are the more impressive because they do not curl back like their *L. pardalinum* parent, the petals being more likely to point out and up. A few fine selections have been made from this cross:

Peachwood As its name suggests, this is a pleasing peach colour. It is best in semi-shade where the colour is not so vulnerable to sun bleaching. This is the mother of 'Lake Tahoe' with *L. bolanderii* as the father.

Rosewood With its graceful flowers, long-petalled and shining pink, 'Rosewood' maintains a demure downward-looking pose but has pointed petal tips fingering the heavens.

Cherrywood This dramatic and stately cultivar is perhaps the most effective of the Bullwood hybrids. Very stylish, large, clean-cut blooms have sharply pointed petals polished to a fine lacquer finish in a crimson-dominated red, but with a gold centre. It grows strongly and makes a most impressive display in mid-summer.

Trumpet Hybrids

For many these are the real lilies. The others may be spectacular and exciting, wonderful flowers and garden plants, but the Trumpets maintain traditional values – a lily should be trumpet-shaped and gorgeously perfumed. The obvious place to start hybridizing may have seemed the easy and beautiful *L. regale* but it proved difficult to cross-breed and, although, of course, it was pressed into service, it was not one of the major influences in breeding the exciting new Trumpets that burst on to a highly appreciative world halfway through this century.

It is true that 'Sulphurgale' was raised in 1913 from *L. sulphureum* × *L. regale* and 'Imperale' was raised from the mating of *L. sargentiae* and *L. regale*, and both were treasured in their time, but most modern hybrid Trumpets are the result of the work of Jan de Graaff and his team with other species. They selected the best forms of the Trumpet species, together with the best of the hybrids, and undertook a large programme of cross-breeding. The species *L. leucanthum centifolium* together with *L. sulphureum* and *L. sargentiae* were crossed both ways with the orange-flowered *L. henryi* with its large turk's-cap flowers. The galaxy of lilies that resulted varied from trumpets, some rather wider than the older types, to flat, star-shaped kinds given the brand name 'Sunburst'. Hybrid lilies of all these types were selected as much for vigour as for beauty. Some of the most important clones and strains are listed here, under the classes into which they are divided.

Trumpet-shaped Hybrids

African Queen Originally, strongly coloured seedlings of trumpet shape from the Golden Clarion strain were carefully interbred to produce a race of richly coloured, funnel-shaped Trumpets that were introduced as the African Queen strain. Subsequently, one particularly outstanding clone was selected and sold as the true 'African Queen' (see page 96). Bulbs of both the clone and the strain are on the market, but the clone seems now to be far more widespread. Huge pyramids of flowers are rich pink-orange in bud and then open to reveal high-gloss petals of warm, glowing orange.

Black Dragon This is a clone selected from a series of white Trumpet hybrids clearly showing the influence of *L. leucanthum centifolium* in its parentage. The buds are a dark wine red, the opened flowers a dazzling snow white.

Black Magic The plants of this strain were originally obtained from the first stem of 'Black Dragon' to bloom. This outstanding seedling was mated with a series of parents, and one mating produced outstanding progeny. The cross was repeated and these seedlings became the Black Magic strain. The flowers are of the same wonderful character as 'Black Dragon', dramatically dark and white.

Damson This remarkable cultivar was a seedling from an aurelian hybrid crossed with a selected form of *L. leucanthum*. It is probably the darkest pink-flowered trumpet. Almost black stems reach 4–5ft (1.2–1.5m) and carry a generous load of large trumpets, well turned back at the mouth. They are a deep beetroot pink with the suggestion of a silvery gloss especially noticeable at the petal ends when the sun catches the blossom.

Emerald This is a large-flowered strain raised from 'Green Dragon' by the pollen of 'Goliath', a large white-trumpeted aurelian. Large, greenish buds split open to reveal white petal surfaces, suffused with lime shades. The sun bleaches the petals but the flowers are glorious in all stages.

Golden Clarion This (see page 97) was the first of the golden-coloured Trumpet strains resulting from the De Graaff team's massive cross-breeding programme. The colours vary between pale and dark yellow.

Golden Splendour This strain (see page 63) of richer-coloured yellow lilies, dark mahogany in bud, with wide golden trumpets, superseded Golden Clarion. They are more-or-less true breeding and are very strong plants making a major impact to the mid-summer garden display.

Green Dragon This was a clone selected as outstanding from among the series of the Olympic hybrids. It has lime-flushed buds and large, open, snow-white flowers.

Limelight The paler hybrids of the Golden Clarion strain were first gathered and offered as the Limelight strain, but later the strain was renamed Golden Dawn and the name 'Limelight' reserved for a single clone, a long-trumpeted, very fine flower with long green buds opening to somewhat hanging trumpets of lime and soft gold. The stems have a lot of narrow, dark foliage.

Mabel Violet This is a strain of very dark pink Trumpets, bred by crossing Pink Pearl with Pink Perfection. A dozen or more flowers, dark maroon in bud, are carried on dark, strong stems. The dark pink of the opened flowers is suffused green in the base and lighter pink at the petal tips.

Moonlight A parallel strain to Golden Splendour, but of lovely greenish yellow colours.

Olympic This strain originally included Trumpets with a wide range of colours, but as now marketed it is restricted to well-formed white Trumpets that may be greenish in bud.

Pink Pearl The strain includes some lovely flowers, normally deep pink in bud but sometimes burgundy, while the opened flowers are soft blush pinks. A little later opening than Pink Perfection.

Pink Perfection The species contributing most to Pink Perfection (see page 67) are *L. leucanthum centifolium* and *L. sargentiae*, with some input from *L. regale*. Although Pink Perfection is marketed as a strain, there appear to be only one or two clones now being used. The standard is a robust plant with an impressive pyramid of from a few to three dozen flowers, each a huge, half-pendent trumpet in very rich beetroot-pink. Stems can be 5–7ft (1.5–2.2m).

Royal Gold This is a golden form of *L. regale*. The flower of the normal form of the species is white with gold restricted to the throat – genetic factors inhibit the spread of the colour. However, in a single *L. regale* plant that grew in Oregon this inhibiting barrier had been overcome and gold had flooded the whole flower. A similar happening occurred elsewhere. What is now sold and grown as 'Royal Gold' is in fact a combination of a few clones.

Sentinel This is a strain of outstanding white Trumpet lilies with perhaps upward of twenty very large flowers on stems 4–5ft (1.2–1.5m) high. Somewhat greenish buds open widely to display sparkling white, wide-petalled flowers with yellow bases. These Sentinels overflow with fragrance.

Bowl-shaped Hybrids

Gold Eagle With flat, outward-facing, deep golden flowers measuring 6–7in (15–18cm) across, this is a fine aurelian kind carrying six or more blooms on stems 4–7ft (1.2–2.1m) high. Slender buds are dark, as is the pollen. The very centre of the flower is green; the petal tips tend to recurve gently.

Heart's Desire The lilies belonging to this strain have attractive wide-flaring flowers in colours from white and cream to yellows, golds, and tangerines. Most are honey-coloured in their bases and paler than the body colour at the petal tips. They have tended to become overshadowed by the trumpet-shaped kinds.

Sunburst Hybrids

These are the widest-opened of the progeny resulting from the mating of *L. henryi* with the various Trumpet species. They are a showy and robust lot. Characteristic of the Sunbursts are their petals, which flare widely from a centre that is often enriched with honey or orange colouring and is marked with the raised points, or papillae, familiar in *L. henryi*. Petal tips may point directly outward or may reflex somewhat. Reflexing can increase as the flower ages. Various colour strains – golden, orange, pink, and silver – have been introduced. They are all well worth growing and impressive, with some blooms reaching 8in (20cm) across.

Bright Star This (see page 68) is the clone that almost single-handed, represents Sunburst hybrids in the market place. It is a robust plant with an arching stem and clean, polished foliage. White, recurving petals form a flower star. An orange stain reaches up from the base to the centre of each petal to form a second star form inside the flower star. A strong bulb can produce a stem topped by an offering of well over a dozen flowers, so that a group of even a few can look very impressive.

White Henryi This is a hybrid from Leslie Woodriff, a Sunburst with all the growing character of *L. henryi*, but with many wide open stars of white painted with honey-orange in the throat and advancing up the petals. To the sides of this coloured area are a series of narrow, rich cinnamon flecks. Its vigour is unabated after a career that started in 1945; it continues to win top honours at American shows. This seems hardly surprising with stems carrying perhaps two dozen or more buds. Height 5–6ft (1.5–1.8m).

Oriental Hybrids

The most exotic and exciting-looking of all the hybrids, with the largest of flowers, the Orientals are refined and graceful as well. The basic cross is between the largest world lily, *L. auratum*, and *L. speciosum*, a favourite pot plant, familiar from in the florist's window. They are Japanese plants, late flowering, and very intolerant of lime. They can have several large heads on strong wiry stems that may need auxiliary help from a stake. Colours are white, pink, and crimson, with sometimes a little gold in the petal centres. Flower shapes are wide shallow bowls, flat stars, or stars with recurving petals. There have been different strains produced in various parts of the world. Particularly fine kinds have evolved in New Zealand and Australia, countries where these lilies grow exceptionally well. Those seen in Britain are usually hybrids bred in the United States or, recently, in Holland. However, one British raiser is now tackling these plants in an energetic manner.

Imperial The Imperial strains with flat-faced flowers were introduced in the 1960s and were for a long time the most often seen of Oriental hybrids. Inevitably they were attacked by virus, but now clean stocks are again available. The Imperials were bred from *L. speciosum* × *L. auratum* with *L. auratum*. The Imperial Silver strain covers the palest forms from this parentage – large shining white flowers with little other colouring evident, though there may be a large number of small crimson dots. In the Imperial Gold strain the ivory flowers are generously banded down each petal centre with gold peppered with crimson spots. At a possible 6ft (1.8m) these plants are likely to be a foot higher than the Silvers. Imperial Crimson flowers have petals that are a deep crimson all over, except for margins of white. The plants stand about 5ft (1.5m). There is another series, Imperial Pink, but these attractive flowers, opening a little earlier, have a slightly different pedigree – *L. speciosum × L. auratum* with *L. auratum × L. japonicum*.

Journey's End A New Zealand-raised cultivar that has spread worldwide. It is a strong-growing kind with plenty of outward-facing, wide flowers with tips slightly reflexed. A very rich crimson pink with white margins and petal tips, darker tones towards petal centres and with lots of deep maroon dots. Excellent in containers. Height 6ft (1.8m).

Stargazer This is an outstanding cultivar (see page 62) grown in larger numbers than any other Oriental hybrid as it is upward facing and makes a first-class cut flower and pot plant. Amateur growers find it equally useful and beautiful; it is a plant of outstanding vitality, of a compact stature, and is generous with its wonderful blossom. Even a very small bulb will produce a fine flowering stem. The shallow, bowl-shaped blooms become flatter as they age. The petals are a very rich crimson with darker spots, while the petal margins are paler. It opens in mid-summer before most of the others, and is one of the finest of lilies for containers.

Casablanca This (see page 34) has huge, shallow, star-shaped blooms, wonderful in their glistening white purity. Very broad petals make an impressive flower that can measure 6–8in (15–20cm) across.

Breeding activity with these Orientals is lively. Large numbers of flowers have been bred and named, either as clones or strains. The Strahm Orientals from Oregon cover a wide range of the possibilities of these hybrids, from pure white to deep crimson. Whenever all the possibilities seem to have been exhausted, new kinds with some special features are introduced.

Yellow Ribbons This highly popular kind has many starry flowers up to 10in (25cm) across glistening white but with conspicuous yellow central bands to each petal. Deeper golden spots and ruffled petal margins enhance the flower, as does the lemony perfume. Height 4–5ft (1.2–1.5m).

Pink Dandy This sturdy, leafy plant has bowl-shaped flowers 9in (23cm) across. From the centre, broad bands of rich pink become narrow toward the petal tips, but the pink is gently suffused to light pink edges while being dotted with darker colour. Height 2ft 6in–3ft 6in (75–105cm).

Snow Gem Of a number of outstanding white-flowered Orientals this is distinguished by size and quality. With good growing it is possible to have blooms measuring 13in (33cm) across, more or less flat with the broad petals waved at the edges and the tips recurving. Opening the palest lemon with lime green nectaries, the petals turn to white but with attractive, even, red spotting. Height 5–6ft (1.5–1.8m).

Royal Splendour Colour and texture make this fluorescent. Broad petals are a uniform rich shining pink with edges lightly crimped and tips gently turned back. The impact of the colour is surprising – the flowers can be seen from considerable distances. They are worth close examination, though, as they are silky smooth and made even more exciting by their bright orange pollen. Height 3ft (90cm).

White Frills This is a free-flowering pure white with sometimes only a few light spots, the petals pointing out widely with much-deckled edges and nectaries green-shaded in youth. Pollen is a brilliant contrast of dark orange and buds are flushed pink. Blooms measure 8in (20cm) across. Height 4–5ft (1.2–1.5m).

The most exciting development in the breeding of these Orientals is the introduction of *L. henryi* blood. This should provide a new race of plants that can be grown in all types of soils, including alkaline ones. Leslie Woodriff produced his 'Black Beauty' from *L. speciosum punctatum × L. henryi* around 1957. It is a very strong plant that will grow in acid and alkaline soils and has a good disease resistance. The mahogany-red flowers have notable green centres and reflexed petals. By colchicine culture a plant was produced with a double chromosome count, 'Tetraploid Black Beauty'. It has larger, very thick-textured, very dark flowers, almost black. It is tolerant of a wide range of pH values on both sides of neutral.

The problem with these fascinating hybrids is the difficulty in breeding from them. There is a sterility barrier. At last a new departure has been made by getting a pink Oriental to set seed to 'Tetraploid Black Beauty'. This newcomer, 'Beauty's Baby' has proved fertile to the pollen of a wide range of Oriental kinds, so it looks as if, at last the dreamt-of possibility of lime-tolerant Orientals has become a reality. 'Beauty's Baby' is a larger flower than 'Black Beauty', with wider petals that are flatter, so making much more of their material. The colour is a full rich one, a shade lighter than that of 'Black Beauty'.

SELECT BIBLIOGRAPHY

Botanical Magazine, Curtis, London, 1790–1934 (At different times many lily species have been illustrated and described.)

Craig, W. N., *Lilies and their Culture in North America*, Langley Prairie, B. C., Chicago, 1928.

De Graaff, J., and Hyams, E., *Lilies*, Nelson, London, 1967

Elwes, H. J., *A Monograph of the Genus Lilium*, London, 1877–1880 (Rare, with hand-coloured illustrations.)

Fox, D., *Lilies*, RHS Wisley Handbook, Cassell/RHS, London, 1985

Fox, D., *Growing Lilies*, Croom Helm, London, 1985

Fox, H. M., *Garden Cinderellas: How to grow Lilies in the Garden*, Macmillan, New York, 1928

Goldring, W., *The Book of the Lily*, The Bodley Head, London, 1905

Grove, A., *Lilies*, T.C. & C. Jack, London, 1911

Grove, A., and Cotton, A. D., *A Supplement to Elwes 'Monograph of the Genus Lilium'*, Dulau & Co., London, 1934–40 (With hand-coloured illustrations by Lilian Snelling.)

Haw, S., *Lilies of China*, Batsford, London, 1966

Jefferson-Brown, M., *Modern Lilies*, Faber & Faber, London, 1966

Jefferson-Brown, M., *Lilies*, David & Charles, Newton Abbot, 1988

Jekyll, G., *Lilies for English Gardens*, Country Life, London, 1901

Macfie, D. T., *Lilies for the Garden and Greenhouse*, Collingridge, London, 1937, 1947

Macneil, A. and E., *Garden Lilies*, Oxford University Press, New York, 1946

Matthews, V., *Lilies*, Kew/Collingwood, London, 1989

North American Lily Society, *The American Lily Yearbooks*, 1939–

Preston, I., *Garden Lilies*, Orange Judd Company, New York, 1929

Rockwell, E. F., and Grayson, E. C., *The Complete Book of Lilies*, Doubleday and Co., New York, 1961

Royal Horticultural Society, *Lily Yearbooks* (subsequently *Lilies*), London, 1933–

Royal Horticultural Society, The International Lily Register, London 1982

Synge, P., *Lilies*, Batsford, London, 1980 (An authoritative review of the genus.)

Stoker, F., *A Book of Lilies*, Penguin, London and New York, 1943

Taylor, G. M., *Lilies for the Beginner*, John Gifford, London, 1947

Wallace, A., *Notes on Lilies and their Culture*, Colchester, 1879

Wilson, E. H., *The Lilies of Eastern Asia*, a monograph, Dulau & Co., London, 1925

Woodcock, H. D., and Stearn, W. T., *Lilies of the World*, Country Life, 1950

SOCIETIES

Australia
Australian Lilium Society, J. H. Young, 24 Halwyn
Crescent, West Preston, Victoria, 3072

Britain
Royal Horticultural Society Lily Group, Vincent
Square, London SW1P 2PE

Canada
Ontario Regional Lily Society, Mrs Gordon Brown,
RR1, Harley, Ontario NOE 1EO
Canadian Prairie Lily Society, Dr E. A. Maginnes, Univ.
of Saskatchewan, Saskatchewan

Germany
Fachgruppe Lilien, Gesellscharft der Stauden-
freunde E V , Martel Hald, Dorrenklingenweg 35,
D 7114 Pfedelbach-Untersteinbach,
W. Germany

Holland
Vereniging 'De Lelie', Wilhelminastraat 45,
Haarlem

New Zealand
Auckland Lily Society, Mrs B. Gross, 34 Maungakiekei
Avenue, Auckland
New Zealand Lily Society, Mr John Gover, PO Box
1394, Christchurch
Otago Lily Society, Mrs D. Aldous, 15 King Edward
Street, Dunedin

South Africa
South African Lily Society, Mrs Eileen Stiemens, PO
Box 3082, Pretoria 0001

United States of America
North American Lily Society Inc., Mrs Dorothy
B. Schaefer, PO Box 476, Waykee, Iowa 50263
Michigan Lily Society, Mrs R. H. Briggs, 21615 Oxford,
Farmington, Michigan 48024
New England Regional Lily Group, Mrs Y. Yeates, 70
Spring Street, Shrewsbury, Mass. 01545
North Star Lily Society, Marsha Hartle, RR4, Box 14,
Owatonna, Minnesota 55060
Ohio Lily Society, Mrs L. Hinman, 29449 Pike Drive,
Chagrin Falls, Ohio 44022

PICTURE CREDITS

INDEX

Numbers in *italics* refer to the captions to the colour plates. **Bold** numbers refer to the main entry in which the species or hybrid is comprehensively described.